Fuel Treatments, Fire Suppression, and Their Interactions With Wildfire and its Effects:

The Warm Lake Experience During the Cascade Complex of Wildfires in Central Idaho, 2007

Russell T. Graham, Theresa B. Jain, and Mark Loseke

I0435126

United States Department of Agriculture / Forest Service

Rocky Mountain Research Station

General Technical Report
RMRS-GTR-229

July 2009

Graham, Russell T.; Jain, Theresa B.; Loseke, Mark. 2009. **Fuel treatments, fire suppression, and their interaction with wildfire and its impacts: the Warm Lake experience during the Cascade Complex of wildfires in central Idaho, 2007**. Gen. Tech. Rep. RMRS-GTR-229. Fort Collins, CO: U.S. Department of Agriculture, Forest Service, Rocky Mountain Research Station. 36 p.

Abstract

Wildfires during the summer of 2007 burned over 500,000 acres within central Idaho. These fires burned around and through over 8,000 acres of fuel treatments designed to offer protection from wildfire to over 70 summer homes and other buildings located near Warm Lake. This area east of Cascade, Idaho, exemplifies the difficulty of designing and implementing fuel treatments in the many remote wildland urban interface settings that occur throughout the western United States. The Cascade Complex of wildfires burned for weeks, resisted control, were driven by strong dry winds, burned tinder dry forests, and only burned two rustic structures. This outcome was largely due to the existence of the fuel treatments and how they interacted with suppression activities. In addition to modifying wildfire intensity, the burn severity to vegetation and soils within the areas where the fuels were treated was generally less compared to neighboring areas where the fuels were not treated. This paper examines how the Monumental and North Fork Fires behaved and interacted with fuel treatments, suppression activities, topographical conditions, and the short- and long-term weather conditions.

Key words: burn severity, wildland urban interface, fire intensity, cold forests

Authors

Russell T. Graham is a Research Forester (Silviculturist) with the U.S. Forest Service, Rocky Mountain Research Station, Moscow, Idaho. His research activities have included the role coarse woody debris plays in forests, large scale ecosystem assessment and planning, describing northern goshawk habitat, and developing forest management strategies (silvicultural systems) for a wide array of management objectives.

Theresa B. Jain is a Research Forester (Silviculturist) with the U.S. Forest Service, Rocky Mountain Research Station, Moscow, Idaho. Her research activities include: understanding how canopy gaps influence forest development, how forest structures and compositions influence both wildfire intensity and burn severity, and how fuel treatments can be designed and implemented to produce desired outcomes.

Mark Loseke is a Fuels Specialist with U.S. Forest Service, Cascade Ranger District, Boise National Forest, Cascade, Idaho. His entire 27-year Forest Service career has been involved with fire, including Fire Management Station Supervisor, Fuels Specialist, and as a Type 1 Burn Boss.

Acknowledgments

First and foremost, we would like to thank the incident management teams and fire crews that managed and worked on the Monumental and North Fork Fires. They provided us with access to the fires while they were burning and many of these individuals provided us with first-hand knowledge of how the fires burned and the suppression tactics they used. Similarly, the fire staffs of both the Boise National Forest and the Cascade Ranger District were outstanding in providing us with flights, ATVs, information, and other help both during and after the fires. In particular Carol McCoy-Brown, District Ranger, Cascade Ranger District; Guy Pence, Aviation and Fire Management Officer, Boise National Forest; Dusty Pence, Fuels Manager, Cascade Ranger District; and the GIS Staff of the Cascade Ranger District deserve special thanks. Also we thank the five reviewers whose excellent suggestions greatly improved our work.

Contents

All photos and figures in the document are of Forest Service origin except where noted.

Preface

During the summer of 2007, wildfires burned over 500,000 acres within central Idaho. Starting in 1996, fuel treatments were implemented to offer protection to over 70 summer homes and other structures located near Warm Lake, approximately 20 miles east of Cascade Idaho. The wildfires of 2007 burned through and around the treatment areas with a variety of intensities, resulting in a variety of burn severities. This paper examines how the Monumental and North Fork Fires behaved and interacted with fuel treatments, suppression activities, topographical conditions, and the short- and long-term weather conditions.

Our research included a combination of site visits both during and after the fires, flights over the terrain, 22 interviews with people assigned to the Monumental and North Fork Fires, and the experiences of employees involved with the fuel treatments and fire suppression activities on the Boise National Forest. In addition, we used information such as, but not limited to, fire progression maps, remote automated weather station (RAWS) data, and daily action plans associated with the Monumental and North Fork Fires. Given all of the factors that influence wildfire behavior and burn severity, the inferences we present are based on the most accurate, unbiased, and complete information available.

Fuel Treatments, Fire Suppression, and Their Interactions With Wildfire and its Effects: The Warm Lake Experience During the Cascade Complex of Wildfires in Central Idaho, 2007

Russell T. Graham, Theresa B. Jain, and Mark Loseke

Introduction

The Payette Crest and Salmon River Mountain ranges of central Idaho create rugged and diverse landscapes. The highest elevations often exceed 10,000 ft with large portions ranging from 5,500 to 6,500 ft above sea level. The Salmon River and its tributaries dissect these mountains creating an abundance of steep side slopes. The South Fork of the Salmon River, with its origin within the 6,000- to 7,000-ft mountains east of Cascade, Idaho, flows north until it joins the main Salmon at an elevation of 2,100 ft. At 5,300 ft, the Warm Lake Basin near the South Fork's origin is one of the many large and relatively flat basins that occur in central Idaho (Alt and Hyndman 1989; Steele and others 1981) (fig. 1).

The climate of central Idaho is influenced by both maritime and continental air masses that produce conditions where frost is possible throughout the year. In addition, in the high and large basins such as Warm Lake, air inversions often occur where warm air traps cool air near the land's surface. The average winter low temperature nears 10 °F and high summer temperatures average 77 °F. However, because of the 7,000-ft elevational relief in central Idaho, a 23 °F temperature differential between the highest and lowest areas can occur at any time. Because of the diverse topography and elevations, precipitation can be highly variable. Approximately 27 inches of precipitation falls within the area with the majority falling as snow from November through March. July and August tend to be the driest months, averaging less than 0.5 inches of precipitation. Annual snowfall totals of 100 inches are common with a wide variety of accumulations. An average of 24 inches of snow covering the valley floors is the norm (Steele and others 1981; WRCC 2008).

The rugged topography and the relatively cool temperatures throughout central Idaho result in subalpine fir (*Abies lasiocarpa*) vegetative complexes defining most forests. Within these forests, subalpine fir can be the dominate tree species with lodgepole pine (*Pinus contorta*), Douglas-fir (*Pseudotsuga menziesii*), and Engelmann spruce (*Picea engelmanii*) as frequent associates due to vegetative succession, fire frequency, insect mortality, and other disturbances. These vegetative

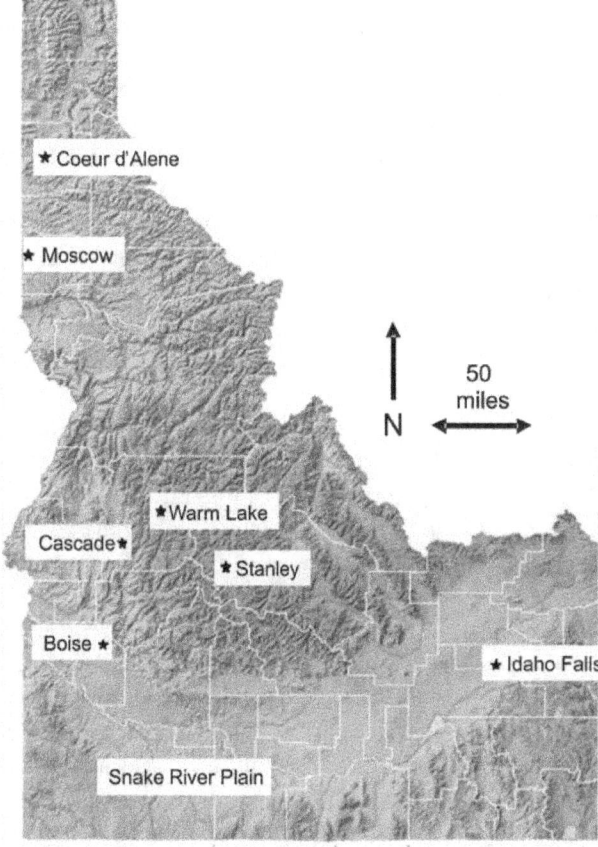

Figure 1. Warm Lake is situated east of Cascade, Idaho, which is located in Valley County in the heart of central Idaho.

USDA Forest Service Gen. Tech. Rep. RMRS-GTR-229. 2009

1

complexes dominate central Idaho. At low elevations (e.g., 5,000-5,500 ft) and on south facing aspects, ponderosa pine (*Pinus ponderosa*), Douglas-fir, and lodgepole pine often prevail. Ground level vegetation includes huckleberry (*Vaccinium* spp.) and false huckleberry (*Menziesia ferruginea*), which can create dense shrub layers to rather depurate layers of grasses (e.g., Idaho fescue, *Festuca idahoensis*) and sedges (e.g., elk sedge, *Carex geyeri*) (Steele and others 1981).

Throughout central Idaho, wildfires shape, rejuvenate, and modify vegetation at variable frequencies and intensities creating an abundance of mosaics occurring at a variety of scales, ranging from small (≤0.25 acres) burned patches to large (thousands to hundreds of thousands of acres) affected landscapes (Crane and Fischer 1986). Wildfires have been a major forest disturbance influencing forest regeneration and development for hundreds if not thousands of years. Additionally, the control of wildfires shaped and impacted land management laws and policies from the beginning of public land management in the United States (Lewis 2005). These policies, especially in the western United States, led to successful and widespread fire exclusion. Minimal fire presence in concert with domestic livestock grazing (or the lack thereof) timber harvesting, and land use (e.g., urbanization, agriculture) tended to simplify, homogenize, fragment, and otherwise modify forest structures and compositions from those that occurred historically (pre-1900) (Graham and others 2004; Steele and others 1981). These changes, along with a lengthening fire season, have contributed to more intense, large, and severe wildfires occurring throughout the United States in recent years compared to fires that burned in previous decades (Dale and others 2001). In 2006, a record 9.9 million acres burned in the United States and a second high 9.3 million acres burned in 2007. Nearly 2.2 million acres burned in Idaho and a large proportion of this burning occurred in central Idaho (NIFC 2008) (fig. 2). Over the past 10 years (1997-2006), an average of 156 wildfires burned on the Boise National Forest, located in southwestern Idaho, changing approximately 17,000 acres (BDC 2007). In contrast, during 2007, 113 wildfires on the Boise burned nearly 347,000 acres or approximately 10 percent of the Forest (BDC 2007). Such fires not only burn trees and other vegetation but they also affect the soil and water resources, wildlife habitat, and in many places homes, lodges, communities, towns, and even large cities (Radeloff and others 2005; Robichaud and others 2000).

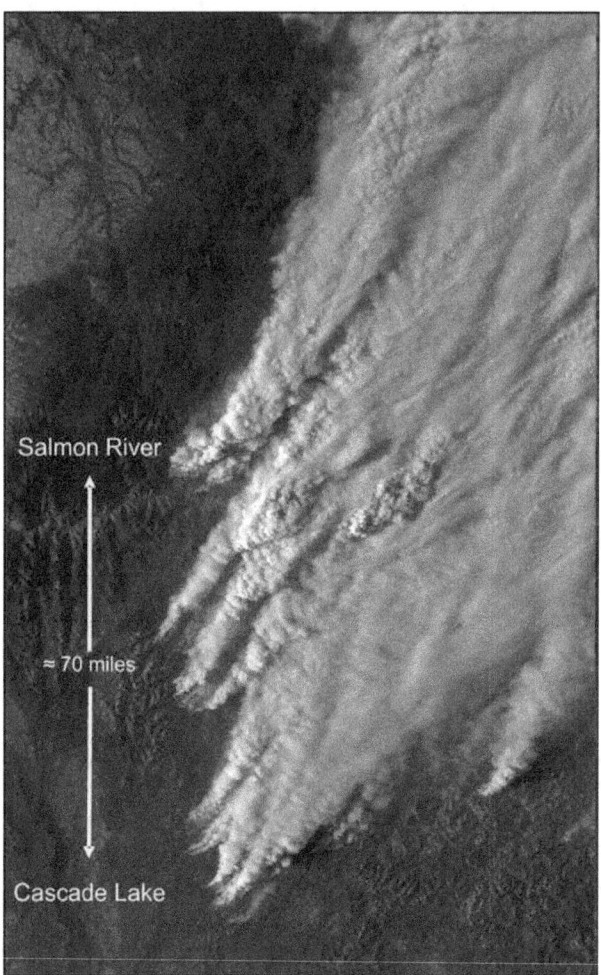

Salmon River

≈ 70 miles

Cascade Lake

Figure 2. A satellite view of smoke from wildfires burning in central Idaho during August, 2007 (http://earthobservatory. nasa.gov/NaturalHazards).

Forest Treatments in the Wildland Urban Interface Near Warm Lake___

A large proportion (>66%) of Idaho lands are owned and/or administered by state and federal governments (NRCM 2008). In addition, there are over 30,000 residences located on lands in the wildland urban interface (WUI) with many of these residences being on lands leased from state or federal governments. Valley County, located in the central part of the Idaho, has over 2,200 residences located in the WUI with a concentration of structures near Warm Lake (Headwaters Economics 2007) (fig. 1). Within the Warm Lake area, approximately 20 miles northeast of Cascade, there are roughly 70 residences and other structures (fig. 3). In addition to the summer homes, the area contains two commercial lodges, two organizational camps, and a Forest Service Project Camp. The Warm Lake Basin is the headwater for the Salmon River, which is home to both Chinook salmon (*Oncorhynchu tshawytscha*) and steelhead trout (*Oncorhynchus mykiss*). Both species are listed as threatened under the Endangered Species Act, which highlights the Salmon River's ecological and commercial value. Because of these threatened species, the amount of vegetative manipulation occurring within the Salmon River drainage since the mid-1970s has been minimal (USDA Forest Service 2003).

In general, owners and residents living near or in forests tend to cherish or favor wildlife, privacy, naturally appearing forests, and recreational opportunities over reducing the risk of their property to wildfire (Kent and others 2003; Monroe and others 2006). Within central Idaho, this trend was exemplified by the homes near Warm Lake, as many were surrounded by dense (2,500 + trees/acre) forests of lodgepole pine and other conifer mixes even though large wildfires had recently burned in the area (figs. 4, 5). The winds driving these fires and winds in general in the Warm Lake Basin tend to blow from the southwest, occasionally from the west, and on rare occasions, winds created by thunderstorms blow from the east and north. The real property, and to a

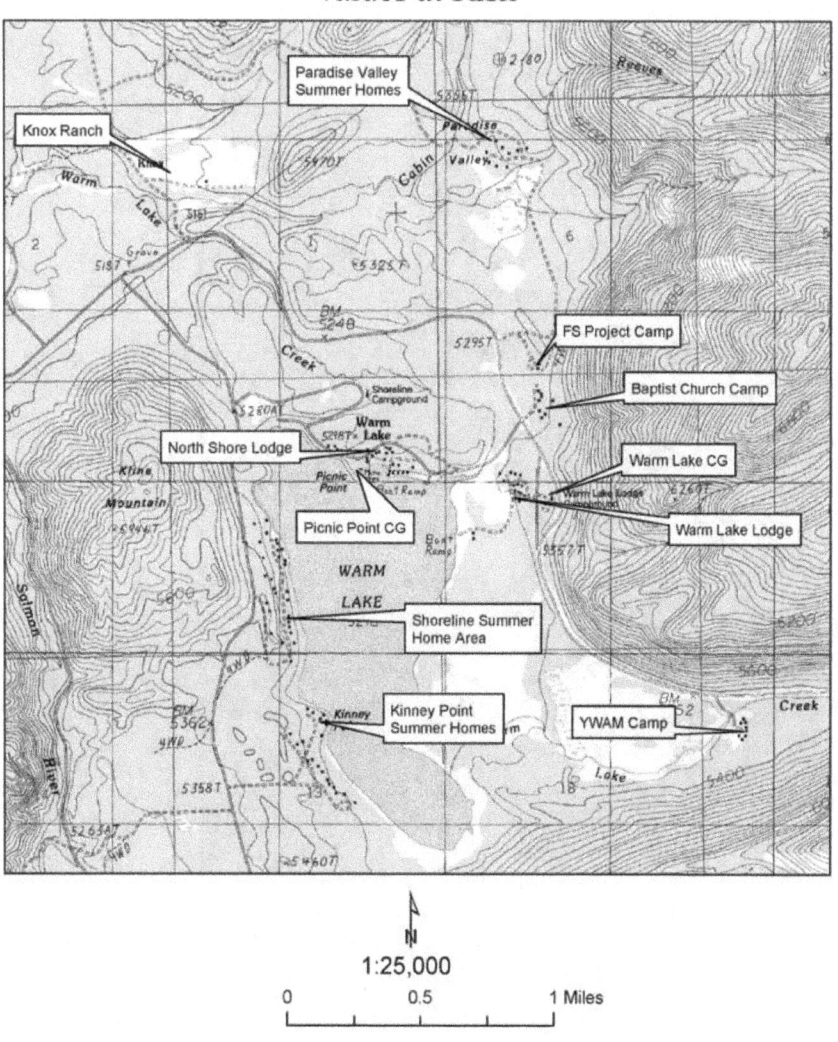

Figure 3. Several homes, lodges, camp grounds (CG), Forest Service camps (FS), and other developments are located within the Warm Lake area of central Idaho.

USDA Forest Service Gen. Tech. Rep. RMRS-GTR-229. 2009

3

Figure 4. A Warm Lake summer home (designated by the arrow) (A) was surrounded by a dense lodgepole pine forest that was treated, significantly reducing the surface, ladder, and crown fuels (B).

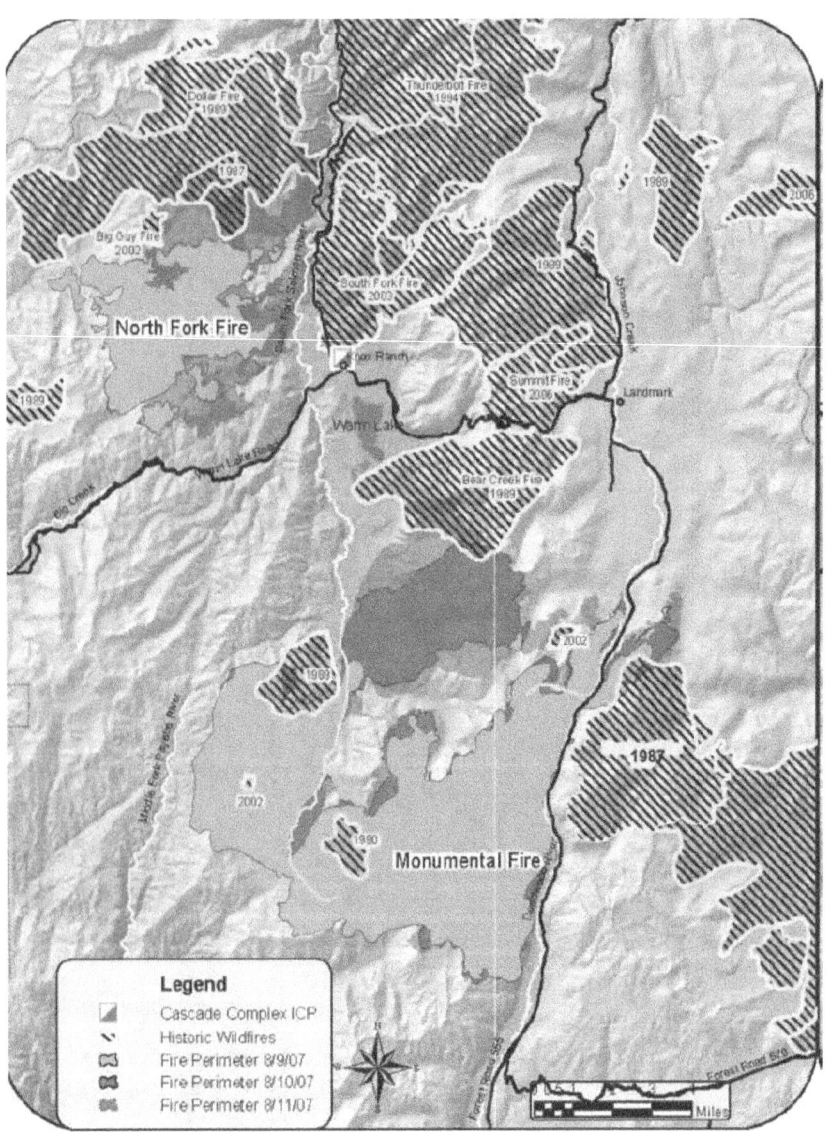

Figure 5. Several large wildfires near Warm Lake burned between 1987 and 2006 that were approached and burned by either the North Fork or Monumental Fire. The Incident Command Post (ICP) of the Cascade Complex was located at Knox Ranch (Bull and others 2007).

limited extent resource values present in the Warm Lake Basin, plus the threat and hazard of wildfire impacting these values, provided the impetus for the Forest Service to plan and execute multiple fuel treatments within and near the basin.

Beginning in 1996, forest treatments were designed and implemented to reduce the risk of a wildfire adversely affecting the structures and other areas of value within the basin. Because the prevailing winds blow from the south and southwest, a priority was to treat fuels west, south, and southwest of residences in the Kinney Point and Shoreline area along the west shore of Warm Lake (fig. 6). In addition to these areas, the fuels south, west, and east of the Paradise Valley summer homes, Forest Service Project Camp, and Baptist Church Camp located northeast of Warm Lake were treated. These fuel

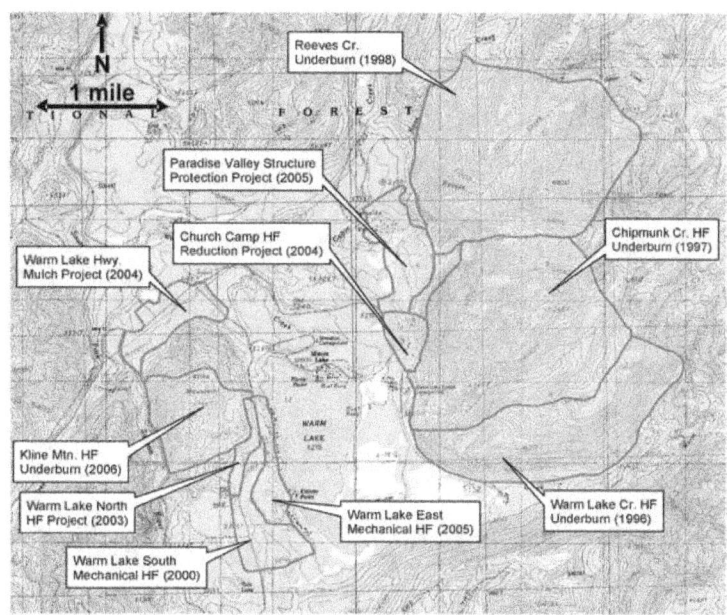

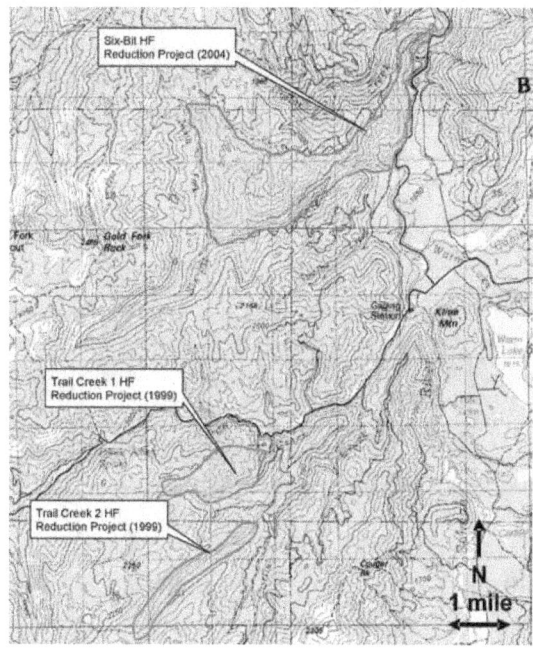

Figure 6. Forest structures and compositions (hazardous fuels – HF) near Warm Lake were modified using both prescribed fire and mechanical methods to modify both wildfire intensity and burn severity if a wildfire was to occur. The treatments were located and designed to offer protection to the many residences and other structures of value near the lake.

USDA Forest Service Gen. Tech. Rep. RMRS-GTR-229. 2009

5

treatments not only offered wildfire protection to these locales, but some protection to the North Shore Lodge, Picnic Point Campground, Youth With a Mission Camp (YWAM), Warm Lake Camp Ground, and the Warm Lake Lodge (figs. 3, 6). Surface fuels, ladder fuels, and crown fuels (in this order of importance) determine both fire intensity and burn severity and strongly contribute to fire resilient forests (Agee and others 2002; Graham and others 2004). With this in mind, the first fuel treatments executed in the basin were aimed at reducing amounts, distribution, and juxtaposition of surface and ladder fuels.

Prescribed fires were the first fuel treatments used in and near the Warm Lake Basin, starting with the Warm Lake Creek Burn in 1996 (fig. 7). Seven burns ranging from 438 acres to over 2,300 acres were conducted, and

by 2006, a total of 8,328 acres were burned (table 1). These fires occurred predominantly in ponderosa pine and Douglas-fir forests located on south and west facing slopes. These burns, for the most part, were aerially ignited using Delayed Aerial Ignition Devices (DAID) or ping-pong balls dropped from helicopters. Some hand ignition (drip torches) occurred near structures (Rauscher and Hubbard 2008) (fig. 7). The fires left a mosaic of forest structures, cleaned the forest floor of litter and fine woody fuels (≤3 inches in diameter), and killed and/or consumed many small trees (≤5 inches in diameter) or ladder fuels.

The Warm Lake south, north, and east projects treated lodgepole pine forests near the cabins along the lake shore (fig. 6, table 2). Similar to the prescribed fires,

Figure 7. Aerial ignition was used for the Warm Lake Creek prescribed fire in 1996. The fuel treatment was located northeast of Warm Lake near the YWAM camp (see figs. 3, 6).

Table 1. Beginning in 1996, prescribed fire was used in and near the Warm Lake Basin to alter the amount, juxtaposition, and distribution of surface and ladder fuels (see fig. 6).

Year	Burn season	Project	Size (acres)
1996	Spring	Warm Lake Creek	480
1996	Spring	Curtis Creek[1]	882
1998	Spring	Reeves Creek	1,636
1997	Fall	Chipmunk Creek	1,958
1999	Spring	Trail Creek	612
2004	Spring	Six-bit Creek	2,342
2006	Fall	Kline Mountain	438
Total acres			8,348

[1] Curtis Creek is located approximately 5 miles west of Warm Lake outside of the Warm Lake Basin.

6

USDA Forest Service Gen. Tech. Rep. RMRS-GTR-229. 2009

Table 2. Mechanical treatments removed standing and down fuels through commercial harvest, mastication (Mast.), slashing (tree falling and cutting), pruning, hand-piling and burning of the piles, and prescribed surface fire (Rx fire). On two occasions mechanical treatments were followed by prescribed fire to further reduce the surface fuels (see fig. 6).

Year	Project	Size	Comm. harvest	Hand slash	Hand prune	Hand pile&burn	Rx fire	Mast.
					Acres			
2000	Warm Lake south	221	221	221	221	221		
2003	Warm Lake north	71	71	71	71	71		
2004	Warm Lake Highway	182						182
2004	Church Camp	110		110	110	95	15	
2005	Paradise Valley	124		124	124	124	124	
2005	Warm Lake east	59		59	59	59		
Total acres		767	292	585	585	570	139	182

these mechanical treatments cleaned the forest floor and removed ladder fuels. In addition, the spacing between tree boles was increased to approximately 10 to 15 ft, thereby increasing the distance between tree canopies. The lower limbs of the residual trees were pruned to a height of 5 ft, further reducing the ladder fuels. The unwanted trees were cut (slashed), as was the material on the forest floor (up to 12 inches in diameter), into lengths that could be hand-piled. All of the cut material was piled and the covered piles were burned either in the late fall or early spring. Because of the urban setting, the burning piles were attended to ensure that the majority (>80%) of the material was consumed to leave a clean and well kept look to the forest floor (fig. 8).

Before treatment

Slash hand piles

Burning slash piles

After treatment

Figure 8. The Warm Lake south mechanical fuel project treated the lodgepole pine ladder and canopy fuels on 221 acres on the west side of Warm Lake. The fuels were slashed, hand-piled, and burned in 2000 (see fig. 6, table 2).

Northeast of Warm Lake, 234 acres of fuels were treated using a variety of mechanical and fire methods (table 2). Around the Paradise valley summer homes, 124 acres of surface and ladder fuels were masticated using a vertical shaft cutting head (fig. 9). After the fuels were mechanically treated, they were burned to further clean the forest floor. The Church Camp project used a combination of mechanical methods and prescribed fire to treat 110 acres of lodgepole pine and mixed ponderosa pine/Douglas-fir forests. Near the cabins, the predominantly lodgepole pine fuels were slashed and hand-piled and the residual trees pruned. After slashing, approximately 15 acres of the surface fuels in the ponderosa pine/Douglas-fir forests were burned (fig. 10). Both of these treatments not only provided protection to the summer homes and camp cabins, but afforded some protection to the Forest Service Project Camp located nearby (fig. 3).

Mastication was also used to treat the lodgepole pine forest along the Warm Lake Highway on the north side of the lake (table 2, figs. 6, 11). One-hundred and eighty-two acres of lodgepole pine trees were thinned and the material masticated using a vertical shaft machine. The chips and chunks were spread across the forest floor creating conditions similar to those produced in the forests

Pre-treatment forest

Post-treatment forest

Figure 9. Surface and ladder fuels on 124 acres in Paradise Valley were treated with a vertical shaft masticator and subsequently burned (see fig. 6, table 2).

8

USDA Forest Service Gen. Tech. Rep. RMRS-GTR-229. 2009

Forest conditions prior to treatment   **Forest conditions after treatment**

Figure 10. Predominantly ladder and surface fuels (110 acres) near the Church Camp were slashed, the material near the cabins hand-piled and subsequently burned, and 15 acres of the slashed fuel were treated with prescribed fire (see fig. 6, table 2).

around the homes on the west side of the lake (fig. 8). Even though the treated area was not exactly adjacent to the North Shore Lodge or Knox Ranch, this treatment was designed to disrupt the progress of a fire if one was to approach either of these areas from the west. Contrary to the other areas masticated, no additional prescribed fire was used (fig. 11).

From 1996 through 2006, a total of 9,095 acres was treated within and near the Warm Lake Basin (tables 1, 2). The treatments were designed to improve protection of the numerous summer homes and other structures that exist around Warm Lake and affect wildfire behavior on 10,000 to 12,000 acres. The projects cost approximately

$1,643,600, or $181 per acre. Most treatments were funded by the Forest Service and occured on Forest Service lands. However, the Paradise Valley and Church Camp projects were funded with Resource Advisory Committee funds. The fuel treatments near Warm Lake, especially around the homes, significantly changed the character of the forests (figs. 4, 8-11). In addition, the surface fuels, which are a major determinant of wildfire ignition and spread, were reduced in all of the areas mechanically treated and on over 8,000 acres that were burned with prescribed fires. Even though the treatments were conducted for the advent of a wildfire, no one expected the treatments to be tested to the degree they were during August of 2007.

Lodgepole pine forest before treatment   **Lodgepole pine forest after treatment**

Figure 11. Surface, ladder, and some canopy fuels were treated along the Warm Lake Highway using a vertical shaft masticator. No additional treatments were applied to the surface fuels (see fig. 6, table 2).

USDA Forest Service Gen. Tech. Rep. RMRS-GTR-229. 2009

9

2007 Wildfire Season in Central Idaho

As noted, the amount of precipitation that falls in the mountains of central Idaho is highly variable. However, beginning in the fall of 2006 and continuing into the spring of 2007, precipitation tended to be about 50 percent of the long-term averages reported by several Idaho weather stations (e.g., Boise, Cascade, Stanley) (WRCC 2008) (fig. 1). With this reduced precipitation, the snow pack for the winter of 2007 was also below the long-term average (1971-2006) within the Warm Lake Basin (NRCS 2003, 2008). Over the last few decades, by mid-April about 35 inches of water, on average, accumulates in the form of snow within the basin and the snow pack often persists until mid-June. However, during the winter of 2007, only 25 inches of water accumulated in the form of snow and was gone by the first of June, deepening the already droughty conditions (fig. 12). Dry conditions prevailed throughout the spring and summer and in several central Idaho locales (e.g., Cascade, Boise, Stanley) monthly precipitation amounts were 40 to 100 percent below their long-term averages (fig. 1). During July and August 2007, southern and central Idaho experienced an abnormal number of hot days with many exceeding 100 °F with minimal rainfall (WRCC 2008). As a result, by April 2007 a moderate drought existed in central Idaho. By May it was severe, and by July it was extreme (fig. 13) (Heim 2002).

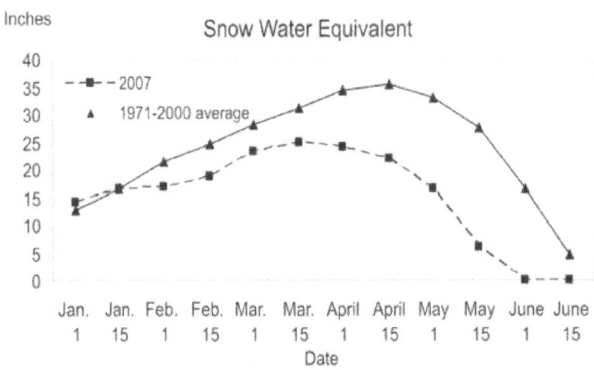

Figure 12. The 2007 snow pack near Warm Lake was below the long-term average as recorded at the Big Creek Summit National Resources Conservation Service SNOTEL site located approximately 5.7 mi west of Warm Lake (NRCS 2003).

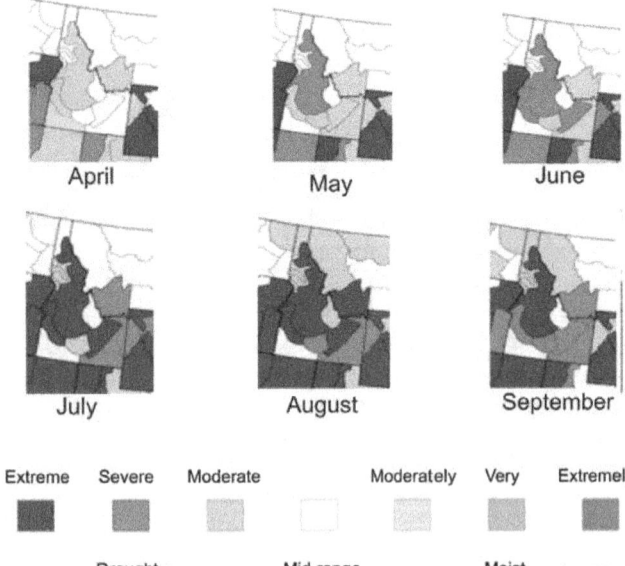

Figure 13. The drought within central Idaho was noticeable by April of 2007, severe by May, and extreme by July as depicted by the Palmer Drought Index (Heim 2002, http://www.ncdc.noaa.gov/oa/climate/research/drought/palmer-maps/).

10

USDA Forest Service Gen. Tech. Rep. RMRS-GTR-229. 2009

As would be expected with the low and early departure of the snow pack combined with dry conditions, the moisture concentrations of the dead 100 hour fuels (≥1.0<3.0 inches diameter) throughout central and southern Idaho were less than 5% by the first of July and the moisture concentrations of the dead 1000 hour fuels (≥3.0 inches diameter) were below 10% (Brown 1974; Brown and others 1985). By mid-July, the moisture concentrations in the large fuels also dropped below 5% in southern Idaho and by July 24, they were below 5% in central Idaho. Consequently, both the weather and fuel conditions resulted in a high fire danger in the region that persisted throughout much of July and very high and extreme fire danger was observed by mid-August. In addition, unstable air masses frequented the area during July and August as measured by the Haines Index, with several days experiencing dry and unstable air occurring low in the atmosphere (Haines 6, fig. 14).

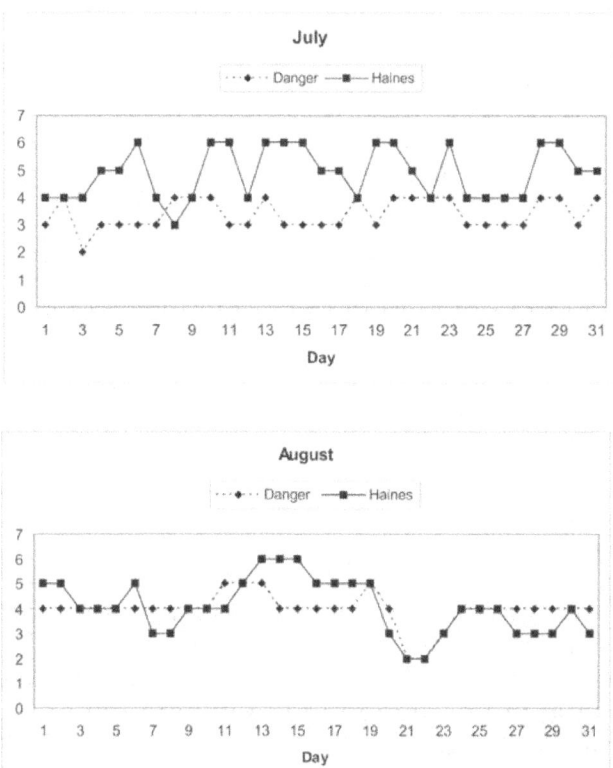

Figure 14. By July, the fire danger in southwestern and central Idaho was high (3) or very high (4) for most of the month and this trend continued in August with extreme (5) fire danger occurring by the middle of the month. In addition, the air masses over the region were relatively unstable as indicated by the Haines Index. The Haines Index can range between 2 and 6. The drier and more unstable the lower atmosphere is, the higher the index.

By late June and early July of 2007, several large wildfires were burning in northern Nevada. By mid-July, over 500,000 acres had burned on the Snake River plain in southern Idaho (fig. 1). The Boise National Forest, located in central and southwestern Idaho, is accustomed to robust fire seasons and has considerable resources to fight wildfires, including local helicopters, engines, and highly trained crews, as well as access to regional and national resources. Similar fire organizations occur throughout the United States and the number of fires and the amount of area burning in the United States by the middle of July, 2007, overwhelmed these available resources that required assets to be shifted and prioritized as new fires were ignited.

Confounding the high and extreme fire danger present throughout much of central and southern Idaho and the scarcity of firefighting resources locally, regionally, and nationally, was a series of thunderstorms that developed in mid-July and moved across the area. A thunderstorm with minimal rain occurred on July 17, igniting over 25 fires on the northern part of the Boise National Forest and several on the adjacent Payette National Forest. The Boise National Forest triaged which fires had priority depending on values at risk and two-thirds of these fires were staffed by July 18. Nevertheless, the Monumental Fire near the headwaters of the South Fork of the Salmon River escaped suppression efforts (fig. 15). This fire, located some 10.5 miles south of Warm Lake, and additional fires (i.e., Riordan, Sandy) burning in the Warm Lake vicinity exceeded local fire fighting capabilities. To manage these fires, two Type 2 Incident Management Teams (IMT2) and one Fire Use Management Team (FUMT) were ordered and assumed responsibility for these fires on July 20. On July 21, the Yellow Fire was discovered west of the Monumental Fire and grew rapidly, ultimately merging with the Monumental Fire (fig. 15). The same lightning storm that ignited the Monumental Fire started the North Fork Fire that was discovered on July 25, approximately 8.8 miles northwest of Warm Lake (fig. 15). Even though it was located on the Boise National Forest, it was assigned to the East Zone Complex of fires burning on the southern part of the Payette National Forest (Bull and others 2007).

Wildfire and Fuel Treatment Interactions Near Warm Lake _____

The basin, in which Warm Lake sits, generally extends from Cabin Peak northeast of Warm Lake to Monumental Peak some 20 miles to the south. A difference of over 3,000 ft in elevation occurs between the peaks and mountain ranges that circumscribe the basin and its floor

USDA Forest Service Gen. Tech. Rep. RMRS-GTR-229. 2009

11

Figure 15. The Warm Lake Basin (outlined) is flanked by peaks over 8,000 ft in elevation on the east and in the range of 7,500 ft on the west. The basin narrows as the South Fork of the Salmon River exits the basin at nearly 5,100 ft above sea level. Both the North Fork and Monumental Fires were ignited by a dry lightning storm on July 17, 2007. The Monumental Fire was discovered on July 19 and the North Fork Fire on July 25. An automated snow content recorder (SNOTEL) is located at Big Creek summit. A permanent remote automated weather station (RAWS) is located north of Warm Lake and two temporary RAWS were established for the fires.

near Warm Lake (fig. 15). This topography lends to the development of air inversions that trap cool air near the land's surface (fig. 16).

At the time the Monumental and North Fork Fires were burning, the fuels in the Warm Lake vicinity were extremely dry. Dead 1000 hour fuel moisture concentrations averaged 9%, dead 100 ($\geq$1.0< 3.0 inches) hour fuel concentrations averaged less than 6%, as did the moisture concentrations of the 10 hour ($\geq$0.25< 1.0 inch) fuels (Readings less than 6% do not register on the protimeter used to estimate the fuel moisture concentrations.). Similar to the dead fuels, the live fuel moisture concentrations, determined by using a COMPUTRAC moisture analyzer, were also very low for the beginning of August. For example, the moisture concentration of elk sedge, a grass-like perennial 8 to 20 inches tall, was 108%. The moisture concentration of huckleberry leaves with berries present on the shrubs was 238%, and the moisture concentration of lodgepole pine and Douglas-fir needles were 106 and 113% respectively. With the exception of the moisture concentration of the huckleberry shrubs, the other live fuel moisture conditions were extremely low and reminiscent of moisture concentrations of those occurring late in the fall when leaves turn color and begin dropping from deciduous plants and the conifers enter dormancy.

Figure 16. Air inversions are common in central Idaho where cool air and smoke in the valleys are trapped by warm air above. These inversions of different strengths often last well into the afternoons.

The fires in and around the Warm Lake Basin increased in size and complexity and, by August 1, over 40,000 acres had burned. For the next 10 days, the Monumental Fire, often driven by strong winds and supported by many days with single digit relative humidity readings, continued burning in a northerly direction toward Warm Lake (figs. 15, 17). The North Fork Fire, driven by the same windy and dry conditions with peak wind gusts exceeding 40 mi/hr, tended to move to the east and northeast. In addition, on August 9, the Monumental Fire made one run 5 miles to the northeast and a second run 1½ mi to the north (fig. 15). In addition to these two fires, the Sandy and Riordan Fires located to the east of Warm Lake continued to burn aggressively, potentially impacting the Warm Lake area and its inherent property and resource values from all directions (fig. 15). The forest treatments aimed at minimizing the impacts from unwanted fire in the area would be put to the test in earnest beginning on August 12.

August 12

August 12, 2007, was considered a Red Flag Day by the Monumental Fire Meteorologist, predicting low air relative humidity, high air temperatures, and gusty winds (table 3). As the Monumental Fire was burning south and east of Warm Lake, the North Fork Fire was burning north and west of the lake, and for the most part since its start, it burned to the northeast away from the lake. However, by August 12, it was burning down slope toward the South Fork of the Salmon River (fig. 18).

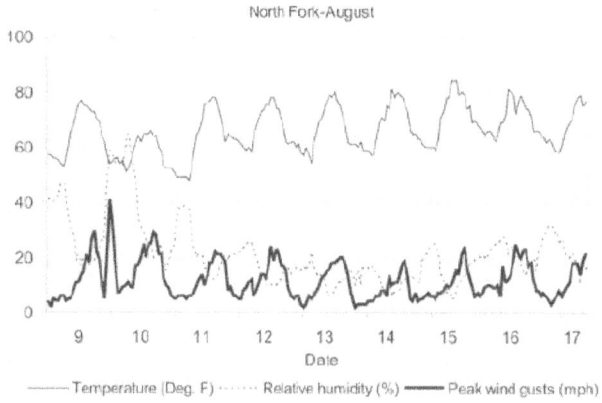

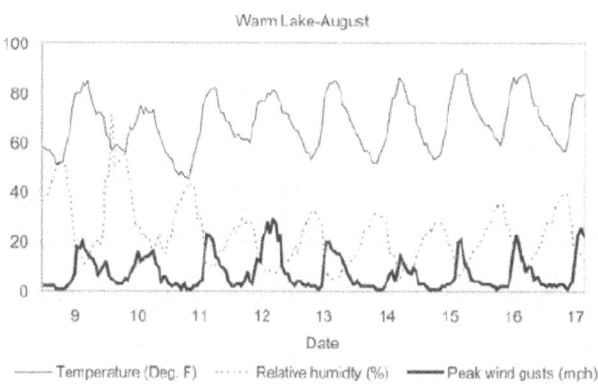

Figure 17. As the Monumental and North Fork Fires approached Warm Lake, wind gusts were strong, air relative humidity was low, and air temperatures were high as recorded by the North Fork and Warm Lake Remote Automated Weather Stations (RAWS) that were established for the fires.

USDA Forest Service Gen. Tech. Rep. RMRS-GTR-229. 2009

13

Table 3. Several weather and fire behavior characteristics were observed and predicted by Meteorologists and Fire Behavior Analysts assigned to the Cascade Fire Complex and recorded by the Tea Pot Remote Automated Weather Station (RAWS) located approximately 18.5 miles north of Warm Lake at an elevation of 4,400 ft above sea level (see fig. 15).

Weather/fire behavior characteristic	Day of month – August, 2007						
	12	13	14	15	16	17	18
	Observed fire weather						
Wind direction[1]	SW	W-SW	SW	S-SW	W-NW	SW	SW
Wind gusts (mph)[2]	31	29	20	36	23	27	31
Relative humidity (%)[3]	8	7	8	12	11	11	9
Temperature (°F)[4]	86	88	90	91	90	85	83
	Predicted fire weather and fire behavior characteristics						
Haines index[5]	5 mod	5 mod	4 low	6 high	4 low	6 high	5 mod
Predicted wind gusts (mph)[6]	30-40	to 30	15-20	15-20	to 20	to 30	to 35
Probability of ignition (%)[7]	85	90	95	90	80	80	85
Spotting distance (miles)[8]	1.0	1.0	0.5	0.75	0.5	1.0	2.0
Crowning potential[9]	Ex	Ex	Ex	Ex	Ex	Ex	Ex
Burn index[10]	98	79	62	65	65	88	105
Energy release component[11]	85	90	88	89	89	85	90
Fire weather watch[12]	N	N	N	TS	TS	TS	N
Fire weather warning[13]	RF	N	N	N	RF	RF	RF
Inversion strength[14]	S	W	S	S	W	W	W
Inversion mixing time[15]	1100	1100	1400	1300	1000	1000	1100

[1] Dominant wind direction occurring late morning through evening (N = north, E = east, S = south, W = west).

[2] Maximum wind gust observed.

[3] Lowest relative humidity observed.

[4] Highest temperature observed.

[5] Haines index indicates atmosphere instability with 4 being low and 6 being highly unstable air occurring near the terrain surface.

[6] Wind gust speed predicted by the meteorologist assigned to the Monumental or North Fork Fires.

[7] Probability of a single fire brand landing and igniting a receptive fuel.

[8] Distance spot fires would l kely be ignited.

[9] Crowning potential indicates the potential for a surface fire to ignite crowns of standing trees (Ex = extreme).

[10] Burn index indicates potential fire intensity. The index divided by 10 provides an estimate of potential surface fire flame lengths.

[11] The energy release component describes the available energy (BTU) per unit area (ft^2) within the flaming front at the head of a fire that is modified by both dead and live fuel moisture concentrations.

[12] No (N) watches and thunderstorm (TS) watches were issued between August 12 and 18.

[13] Red Flag (RF) warnings for gusty winds, high temperatures, and low relative humidity were issued (N = No).

[14] Strong (S) and weak (W) air inversions were predicted for the Warm Lake Basin where warm air traps cooler air near the terrain's surface.

[15] Time of day when the air inversion was predicted to lift.

During the morning of the 12th, a strong air inversion covered the basin, trapping cool air and smoke, which in turn decreased fire intensity (fig. 16). During the inversion, Monumental Fire crews burned the surface fuels ¼ to ½ miles south from Kinney Point between Road 427 and the lake shore (figs. 6, 18, 19). This burning took place in the Warm Lake south and portions of the Warm Lake east fuel treatment areas consuming the small amount of surface fuels present (figs. 6, 19, table 2). These activities were designed to offer additional protection to that already provided by the fuel treatments to the summer homes in the Kinney Point area as the Monumental Fire approached (figs. 3, 15, 18, 19).

When the inversion lifted at approximately 1100 hours, winds were predicted to gust between 30 and 40 miles per hour, crowning potential was to be extreme, and the Burn Index predicted surface fire flame lengths over 9 ft (table 3). On August 12, the three RAWS providing weather information to the fires recorded wind gusts over 29 miles per hour, with most winds blowing from the southwest (table 3, figs. 15, 17). As predicted, air humidity readings at the three RAWS were less than 10% and air temperatures exceeded 80 °F by mid-afternoon. These conditions caused considerable crowning as the fire moved east up Camp Creek to the southeast of Warm Lake. In contrast, the areas southwest of Warm Lake that

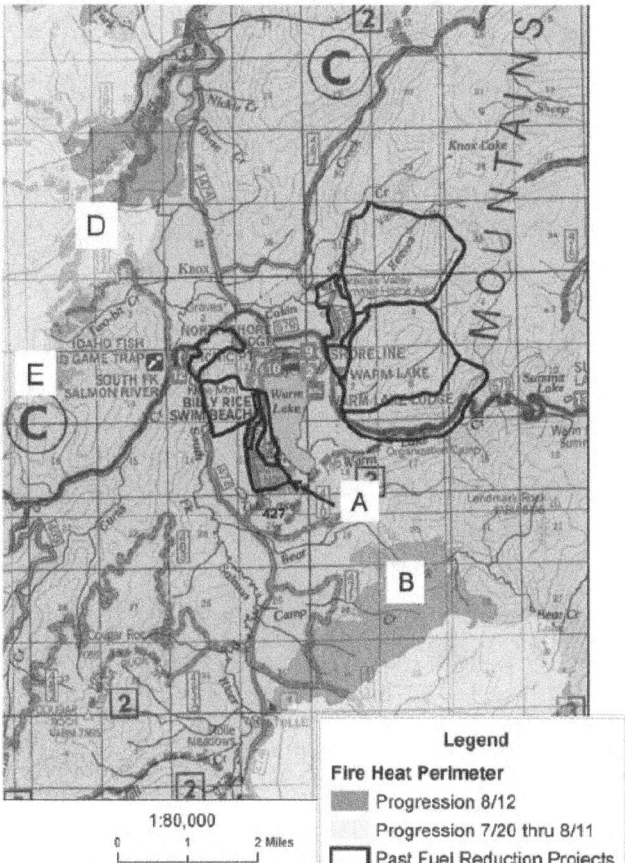

Figure 19. A Monumental Fire crew burned the surface fuels on August 12 in the Kinney Point area on the west side of Warm Lake where both the surface and canopy fuels were treated in 2000 or 2005. Note the burning is occurring in the morning when the air inversion is in place (see fig. 6).

Legend

Fire Heat Perimeter
- Progression 8/12
- Progression 7/20 thru 8/11
- Past Fuel Reduction Projects

1:80,000
0 1 2 Miles

Figure 18. On August 12 a Monumental Fire crew burned the surface fuels within the treatment areas on the southwestern edge of Warm Lake (A) and the Monumental Fire burned into both the Bear and Camp Creek drainages (B). The North Fork Fire tended to burn toward the northeast (D) with some burning occurring down slope toward the Warm Lake Highway and the South Fork of the Salmon River (E).

were treated and subsequently burned by a Monumental Fire crew on the morning of the 12th only experienced several spot fires that were easily suppressed after the flaming front subsided. On August 12, the Monumental Fire burned about 1,200 acres and became well established in both Bear and Camp Creek drainages some 1½ to 2 miles southeast of Warm Lake (fig. 18).

August 13

During the early morning of August 13, the inversion developed in the basin and air temperatures dropped briefly to low as 54 °F and relative humidity approached 20% (fig. 17). Similar to the previous day, predicted crowning potential was extreme, potential spotting

distances were a mile, and wind gusts up to 30 mi/hr were predicted (table 3). In contrast to August 12, the inversion was weak, which allowed the winds and temperatures to increase early in the day and the relative humidity of the air to decrease to single digits earlier and remain there longer. Wind gusts to 20 mi/hr were observed at both the Warm Lake and North Fork RAWS and wind gusts to 29 mi/hr were recorded at the higher elevation Teapot RAWS (table 3, fig. 17). These gusts, and winds in general, blew out of the south and southwest throughout the basin and within the surrounding mountains. By mid-afternoon on the basin floor, air temperatures exceeded 80 °F and its relative humidity was 5%. Similarly, at Teapot, the air temperature was nearly 90 °F and its relative humidity was 7%. Needless to say, these weather conditions and the topographic position the Monumental Fire achieved in the lower and southern portions of the Bear and Camp Creek drainages set the stage for intense wildfire behavior.

Because of the weak inversion on August 13, intense fire activity within both the Camp and Bear Creek drainages started early in the day. Pushed by southwesterly winds that aligned perfectly with the topography, the Monumental Fire burned the majority of both watersheds by 1600 hours (fig. 20). The fire not only burned to the northeast approximately 5 miles, but, moved into the Warm Lake Creek drainage directly east of Warm Lake. Driven by hot, dry, and strong southwesterly winds, the Monumental Fire, with 100- to 200-ft flame lengths, burned the entire Warm Lake Creek drainage (fig. 21). As it was burning, it moved through the 480 acres located on the north side of

USDA Forest Service Gen. Tech. Rep. RMRS-GTR-229. 2009

15

Figure 20. On the east side of Warm Lake, the Monumental Fire burned the entire Camp and Bear Creek drainages on August 13.

Figure 21. Monumental Fire produced a large smoke column (A) as viewed from Knox Ranch as the fire ran to the northeast on August 13 and burned the entire Warm Lake Creek drainage (B).

Warm Lake Creek that were treated with prescribed fire in 1996. In addition, the fire burned the northerly aspect directly across from the Warm Lake prescribed fire that was previously burned by the Bear Creek Fire of 1989 (fig. 22). Situated between these two side-slopes in the bottom of the Warm Lake Creek valley is the Youth With a Mission Camp (YWAM) (figs. 3, 22).

The exact timing of when the fire passed the YWAM Camp is unknown, but it was most likely in the late afternoon or early evening. Immediately to the south of the camp, in the area that was burned by the 1989 Bear Creek Wildfire, the Monumental Fire burned intensely, consuming the majority of both the live and dead vegetation (figs. 22, 23). In contrast, the burning that was north of the camp on the south facing slope was far less intense, leaving much of the vegetation intact (fig. 23). Multiple cabins are spread throughout the

YWAM Camp with large trees nearby (fig. 24). Prior to the fire approaching the camp, the grounds were wetted using sprinklers and they continued to sprinkle until a large (20+ inches in diameter) Engelmann spruce within the compound toppled, disrupting the irrigation. The fire on the north facing slope burned with such intensity that an Engelmann spruce located next to a cabin within the compound ignited at least 20 ft above the ground surface and ultimately torched the remainder of the tree crown above (fig. 24). However, there was minimal surface fire in the camp that was easily extinguished by fire crews when the flaming front(s) had passed.

Figure 22. On August 13 the Monumental Fire burned through the Warm Lake Creek (1996) prescribed fire area (A), spotted into the Warm Lake east and south project areas where the surface fuels were burned on August 12 (B) (see fig. 19), burned through the area charred by the Bear Creek Fire of 1989 (C), and became fully established in the South Fork of the Salmon River near Stolle Meadows (D).

Figure 23. The Monumental Fire burned intensely on the north facing slope adjacent to the Youth With a Mission (YWAM) Camp and consumed a large portion of the of the dead fuels remaining after the 1989 Bear Creek Fire and most of the live vegetation that developed (see fig. 3) (A). In contrast, the fuels that were treated with prescribed fire in 1996 on the south facing slope (B) burned rapidly, but the intensity was lower than that exhibited by the fire on the north facing slope.

USDA Forest Service Gen. Tech. Rep. RMRS-GTR-229. 2009

17

Figure 24. Large trees often adjoined the cabins in the Youth With a Mission (YWAM) Camp. The Monumental Fire when it passed the camp, did so with sufficient intensity to ignite the crown of this Engelmann spruce some 20 ft above ground level.

On August 13, the Monumental Fire burned to the north, primarily staying on the east side of Roads 474 and 427 (fig. 22). The fire burned into the areas on the west side of Warm Lake where the fuels were treated in 2000 and 2005, and the surface fuels were subsequently burned by Monumental Fire crews on the morning of August 12 (figs. 18, 19). The fire stayed on the east side of Road 427 as it approached Kinney Point area, and only spot fires were ignited where the fuels had been treated and they were easily suppressed by fire crews (fig. 22). Even though the fire mostly stayed on the east side of Road 474, it again established itself in a key topographical position for future burning — the west side of Road 474 near Stolle Meadows (fig. 22). Approximately 5,800 acres were burned by the Monumental Fire on August 13.

August 14

On August 13, a noticeable amount of burning by the North Fork Fire occurred in the Two Bit Creek drainage just northwest of Warm Lake (fig. 25). Realizing that both the South Fork of the Salmon River and the Warm Lake Highway would offer ready made fuel breaks, North Fork Fire crews began burning the untreated fuels located between the fire and the Warm Lake highway, as well as between the fire and the river. These previously untreated areas were burned during the night of August 13 and the morning of August 14 (fig. 26). In contrast to suppression burning (burnout) in areas where the fuels

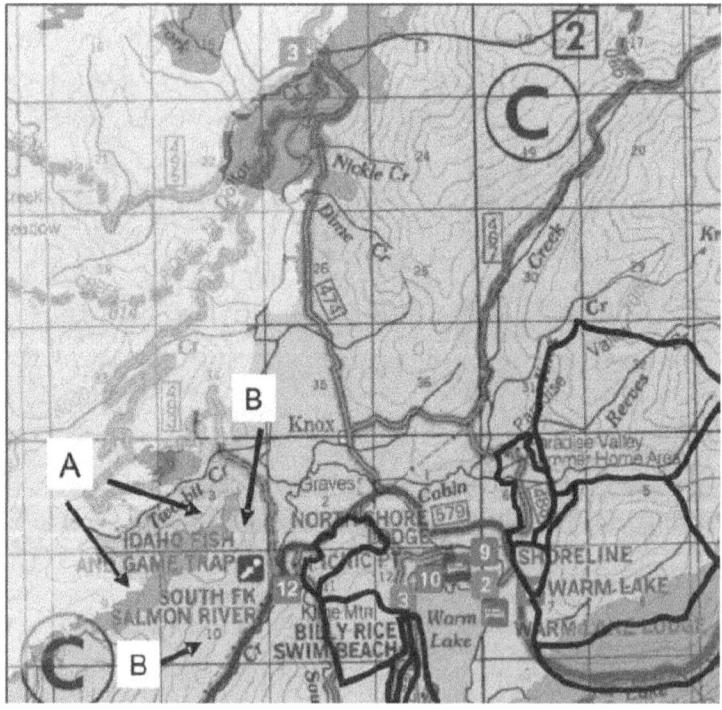

Figure 25. On August 13, the North Fork Fire burned down slope toward the South Fork of the Salmon River and toward the Warm Lake Highway (A). In addition, North Fork Fire crews burned untreated fuels from Two Bit Creek south to the Warm Lake Highway and up toward the advancing fire (B).

USDA Forest Service Gen. Tech. Rep. RMRS-GTR-229. 2009

Figure 26. Torching occurred during burnout operations in the untreated fuels on the west side of the South Fork of the Salmon River (A) (see fig. 25). By 2400 hours on August 13, considerable flaming from the burnout operations was evident as viewed from Knox Ranch (B).

have been treated, burnout operations in untreated fuels can result in more intense fires (figs. 19, 26). This intense burning ignited several spot fires in the forests located to the east toward the river and Knox Ranch (fig. 25).

Once again, a strong air inversion set up during the morning of August 14. Once it lifted, predicted wind gusts were to approach 20 mi/hr, air temperature 90 °F, and relative humidity of the air in the single digits (table 3). The inversion was not expected to disperse until 1400 hours; however, the North Fork Fire Meteorologist issued a weather update at 1245 indicating that air was mixing and the inversion was lifting. By 1300 hours, winds gusting to 20 mi/hr were observed at the North Fork, Warm Lake, and Teapot RAWS (table 3, fig. 17). By mid-afternoon, the hot (≈90 °F) and dry (relative

humidity 5-7%) winds blew from the west (as recorded by the North Fork and Teapot RAWS) instead of prevailing from the south and southwest.

After the inversion lifted, trees were torching within the main North Fork Fire perimeter and in areas where the burnout occurred (fig. 25). This intense fire behavior produced more spot fires on the east side of the South Fork of the Salmon River and south of the Warm Lake Highway (fig. 25). Even though heavy helicopters and several crews attempted to suppress these fires, the North Fork Fire rapidly increased in intensity. As the North Fork Fire was burning northwest of Warm Lake, the Monumental Fire was burning intensely east of the lake along the ridge separating Warm Lake Creek from Johnson Creek (figs. 27, 28). Driven by strong westerly winds, and possibly pulled by winds generated by the plume of the Monumental Fire, the North Fork Fire burned through the Knox Ranch and subsequently burned two uninhabitable structures (fig. 29). The North Fork fire burned through a portion of the area on Kline Mountain that was treated with prescribed fire in 2006 and through the Warm Lake Highway Project area where the ladder and surface fuels had been masticated in 2004 (figs. 6, 11, 27, 28). Even though the North Fork Fire had ample opportunity, it did not burn into the area occupied by the Picnic Point Campground, North Shore Lodge, and other structures located on the north side of Warm Lake (figs. 3, 28). In fact, on August 14 the southern perimeter of the fire tended to be very straight as it burned to the east (fig. 28).

By the end of August 14, the Monumental and North Fork Fires were about 1½ miles apart as they moved to the northeast of Warm Lake and were burning both north and south of the Paradise Valley summer homes (fig. 28). On the 14th, the North Fork Fire burned approximately 1,000 acres within the basin and the Monumental Fire burned an additional 1,200 acres. By burning into the Johnson Creek drainage, the Monumental Fire had traversed approximately 18 miles or nearly the entire length of the Warm Lake Basin (fig. 15).

August 15 and 16

Relatively unstable air was predicted over the basin for August 15 as indicated by the Haines Index (table 3). Similar to the previous day's weather, winds were going to be gusty, air temperatures high, and air relative humidity low. By mid-day, winds were gusting over 35 mi/hr at the Teapot RAWS and the air temperature was over 90 °F. Similarly, on the basin floor, the Warm Lake RAWS recorded air temperatures over 90 °F and the North Fork

USDA Forest Service Gen. Tech. Rep. RMRS-GTR-229. 2009

19

Figure 27. After the inversion lifted on August 14, the North Fork Fire rapidly increased in intensity as it burned to the east. In this view of the fire (A), it had just passed through the area along the Warm Lake Highway where the fuels were masticated as it approached the Knox Ranch (see figs. 6, 11). In addition to be driven by strong winds from the west, the fire may have been pulled by winds created by the Monumental Fire as it burned on the ridge separating Warm Lake Creek from Johnson Creek located to the north (B) (see fig. 28).

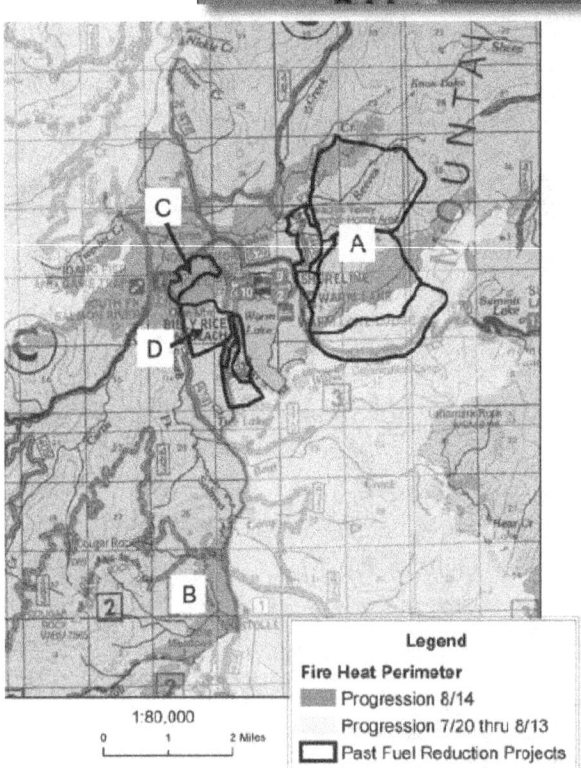

Figure 28. On August 14, the Monumental Fire burned north into the Johnson Creek and Reeves Creek drainages that were burned by prescribed fires (A) and continued to burn in the South Fork of the Salmon River headwaters (B). Driven by dry westerly winds, the North Fork Fire burned to the east through an area where the fuels were treated along the Warm Lake Highway (C) and into areas where prescribed fires occurred on Kline Mountain (D).

Figure 29. Heavy helicopters were used as the North Fork Fire approached the Knox Ranch where the Cascade Incident Command Post was located (A). Within the Knox Ranch, two structures were burned by the North Fork Fire (B).

USDA Forest Service Gen. Tech. Rep. RMRS-GTR-229. 2009

21

Figure 30. Relatively benign fire behavior was exhibited by the North Fork Fire on August 15 and 16 as it burned near the Knox Ranch and Paradise Valley summer homes (arrow).

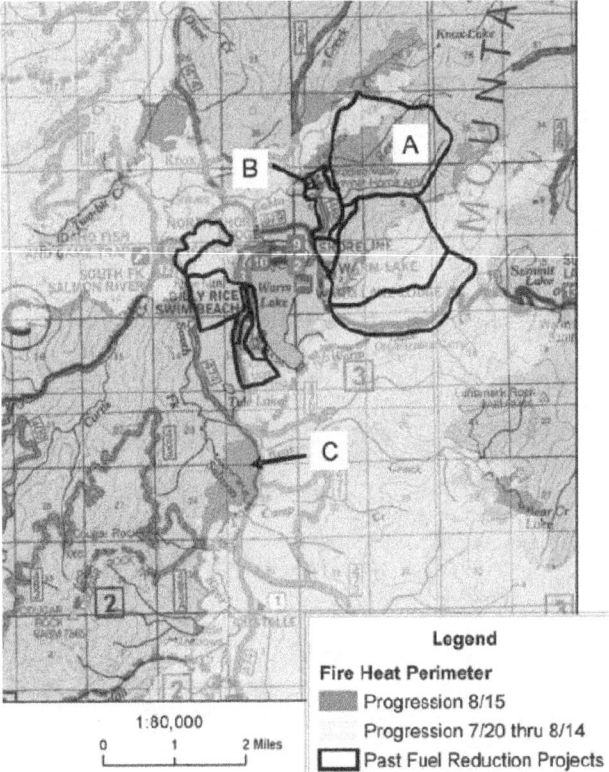

Legend

Fire Heat Perimeter
Progression 8/15
Progression 7/20 thru 8/14
Past Fuel Reduction Projects

1:80,000
0   1   2 Miles

Figure 31. On August 15, the North Fork Fire burned through portions of the Reeves Creek (1998) (A) fuel treatment area and near the Paradise Valley summer homes (B). The Monumental Fire continued to burn along the South Fork of the Salmon River (C).

RAWS recorded air temperatures over 80 °F. Peak wind gusts observed at both RAWS were approximately 20 mi/hr and the air humidity values were less than 6% (fig. 17).

Although the weather was favorable for intense fire behavior, both the North Fork and Monumental Fires did not burn aggressively as previous days. The North Fork Fire continued to burn northeast of Warm Lake as it moved south toward the Paradise Valley summer homes (figs. 3, 30). A portion of this burning occurred in the Reeves Creek drainage where the surface fuels were treated in the spring of 1998 (table 1, figs. 6, 31). The Monumental Fire continued to burn in the Stolle Meadows area south of Warm Lake and burned small areas on its eastern perimeter. In total, on the 15th, the Monumental Fire burned around 750 acres while the North Fork Fire burned approximately 600 acres.

Hot and dry weather continued to prevail on August 16 but the winds, especially those recorded at the Teapot RAWS, tended to blow from the west and northwest. In addition, milder wind gusts were experienced at all of the RAWS than on previous days. This resulted in a predicted fire spotting distance of ½ mile compared to ¾ mile on the previous day (table 3). Also, compared to previous days, the air inversion over the basin on August 16 was weak, allowing air to more readily mix between the high and low elevations. As a result, the intensity of both fires was rather benign, their growth was small, and their perimeters were similar at the end of the day to what they were on August 15 (fig. 31).

August 17

A weak air inversion developed over the basin on the night of August 16 and morning of August 17. This weak inversion allowed winds on the basin floor to gust to over 15 mi/hr by 1000 hours and nearly 20 mi/hr by noon. At 1300 hours, gusts of hot (≈ 80 °F) and dry (≈ 10% relative humidity) winds were approaching 30 mi/hr on the basin floor (fig. 17). Similar to August 15, these weather conditions resulted in a high Haines Index, indicating highly unstable air occurring near the terrain surface and predicted surface fire flame lengths approaching 9 ft (table 3). By mid-afternoon, the Warm Lake RAWS showed the majority of the winds blowing generally from the south while the winds recorded by the North Fork RAWS blew from the west. This Red Flag Day once again set the stage for both the Monumental and North Fork Fires to test the efficacy of the fuel treatments implemented near Warm Lake.

On August 15, a spot fire was apparently ignited on the ridge separating Curtis Creek from the South Fork of the Salmon River, over 2 miles southwest of Warm Lake (fig. 32). This spot fire merged with the main Monumental Fire and the combined fires burned northward. The north/south alignment of the South Fork's topography matched perfectly with the southerly winds to produce intense fire behavior (fig. 33). The fire ignited several spot fires along the west side of Warm Lake, which were readily suppressed in areas where the surface fuels were previously treated. These treatment areas included Warm Lake North, East, and South fuel reduction projects, as well as the areas within these projects that were burned by the Monumental Fire crews on August 12 (figs. 6, 8, 18, 19). The Monumental Fire also burned into areas where the surface fuels were treated on the south, east, and west sides of Kline Mountain in 2006 (figs. 6, 32, 33). On August 17, the Monumental Fire merged with

the North Fork Fire on the northwestern side of Warm Lake and burned approximately 1,400 acres (fig. 32).

The Monumental and North Fork Fires also merged on the northeastern side of Warm Lake as they burned in and around the Paradise Valley summer homes, Forest Service Project Camp, and Baptist Church Camp (figs. 3, 32). The Reeves Creek under burn (1997), and the Paradise Valley (2005), Church Camp (2004), and Chipmunk Creek (1998) fuel treatment areas were either burned through or approached by the fires (figs. 6, 32). As the fires burned, spots were ignited in the mechanical fuel treatments associated with the homes and were quickly extinguished by the North Fork Fire crews (fig. 34). The North Fork and Monumental Fires burned approximately 600 acres on the eastern side of Warm Lake.

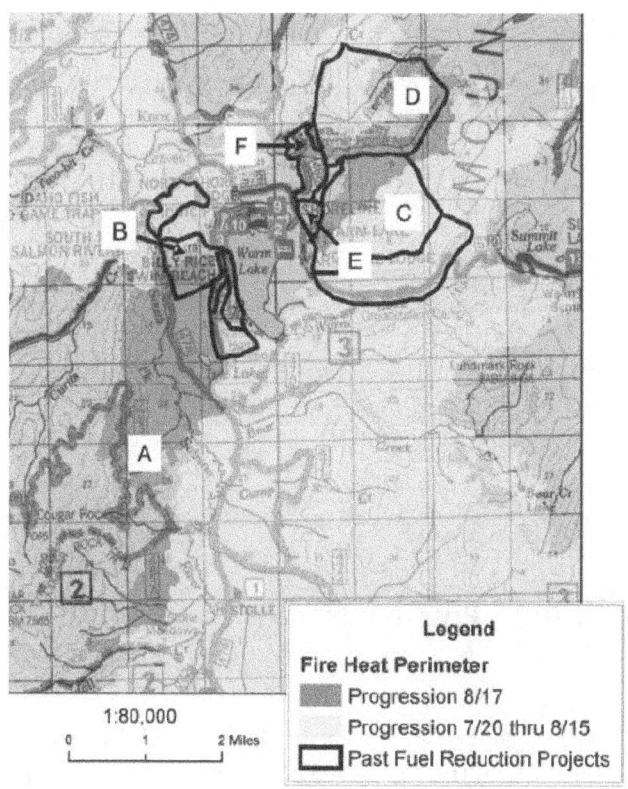

Figure 32. On August 17, the Monumental Fire burning from a spot (A) on the ridge between the South Fork of the Salmon and Curtis Creek aggressively burned to the north burning into the Kline Mountain area in which the surface fuels were burned in 2006 (B). Also, it merged with the North Fork Fire both along Kline Mountain (B) and in the vicinity of the Paradise Valley summer homes (F). The fire(s) in this area burned through or approached the Chipmunk Cr. (C), Reeves Cr. (D), Church Camp (E), and Paradise Valley (F) fuel treatment areas.

Figure 33. On August 17, the Monumental Fire burned intensely as it moved north along the west slope of Kline Mountain (A). More than once, Warm Lake itself served as a safe zone for firefighters (B).

USDA Forest Service Gen. Tech. Rep. RMRS-GTR-229. 2009

23

Figure 34. A spot fire near a cabin in the Baptist Church Camp was readily extinguished by a North Fork Fire crew. Note the open forest condition and the relatively clean forest floor.

August 18 to Snow Fall

On August 18, a Burn Index of 105, one of the highest ever recorded for the Boise National Forest, indicated weather conditions were very favorable for the expansion of the North Fork and Monumental Fires (table 3). Winds continued to be gusty within and near the basin with speeds over 30 mi/hr recorded at the Teapot RAWS. Once again, the relative humidity of the air was in the single digits. On the 18th, the North Fork and Monumental Fires continued to burn rather intensely, with the major burning occurring in the Johnson Creek drainage located to the north and east of Warm Lake. Additionally, to the south and west of Warm Lake, the Monumental Fire burned approximately 600 acres (fig. 35).

The North Fork and Monumental Fires continued to burn in central Idaho until early October when snow finally arrived and brought an end to the 2007 fire season on the Boise National Forest. Over 150,000 acres burned in the vicinity of Warm Lake yet only two rustic buildings were destroyed. The investment in fuel treatments over the previous 11 years appeared to contribute significantly to these results.

Efficacy of Fuel Treatments _____

Physical setting (e.g., topography, elevation, orientation), fuel amounts, structure, composition, moisture content, and the arrangement of each element and its juxtaposition to the start and progression of a fire and suppression activities, along with the long- and short-term weather, determine the intensity and the effect or burn severity of a wildfire (Agee and others 2002;

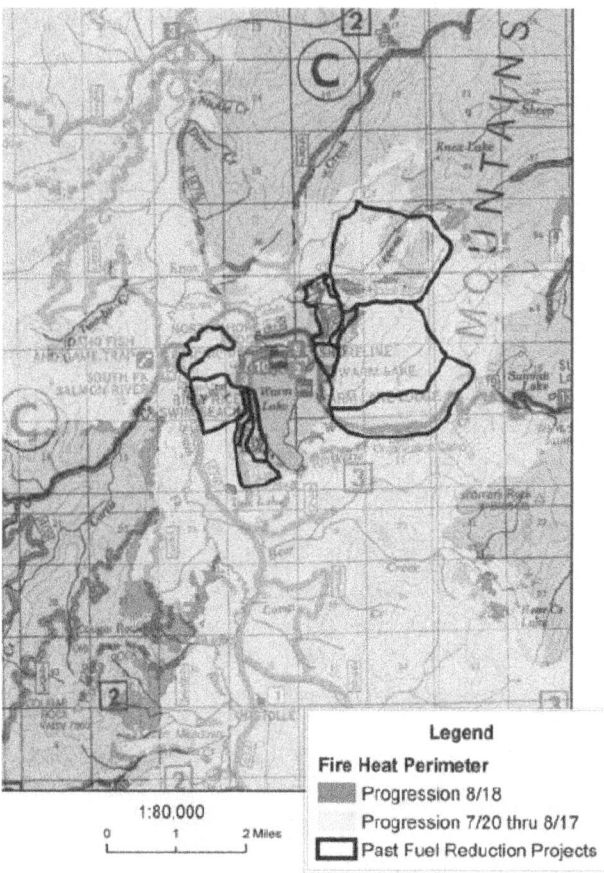

Legend
Fire Heat Perimeter
▨ Progression 8/18
▨ Progression 7/20 thru 8/17
☐ Past Fuel Reduction Projects

1:80,000

0   1   2 Miles

Figure 35. By August 18, the Monumental and North Fork Fires, while burning near Warm Lake, burned through or approached over 5,000 acres (outlined) that were treated to influence both fire behavior and burn severity.

Graham and others 2004; Jain and Graham 2004, 2007). All of these elements and their interactions came into play as the Monumental and North Fork Fires burned near Warm Lake.

Weather, Fuel Treatments, and Suppression

Weak and strong air inversions prevailed over the Warm Lake Basin on most of the days the Monumental and North Fork Fires burned. When warm air aloft traps cool air near the land's surface, air temperatures tend to be cool, relative humidity of the air high, and winds light (figs. 16, 17). Such conditions provided opportunities for Monumental and North Fork Fires fire crews to conduct burnout operations, often within areas where the fuels had been treated (fig. 19). When the inversion lifted and air mixed between the high and low layers, rapid changes in winds, air temperature, air humidity, and resulting fire behavior would occur. Where the fuels had been treated, fire behavior was often noticeably different from that which occurred in neighboring untreated fuels. In addition, the inversion tended to lift at the higher elevations or within the southern part of the basin before the northern or lower portions of the basin. This knowledge and the location of fuel treatments constrained the timing of when burnout operations occurred and also influenced fire suppression activities. For example, when the inversion lifted in the Stolle Meadows area to the south of Warm Lake, air operations personnel on the Monumental Fire planned their activities and estimated when they could operate within other locales near the fire. The timing of the air mixing also predicted when fire intensity would increase, making direct fire suppression difficult. During the inversion, burnout operations in areas where fuels were treated were very effective and created low intensity, easily managed surface fires (fig. 19). In contrast, during the inversion, rather intense fires were often created during burnout operations with the torching and crowning in fuels that were not treated (fig. 26).

Topography, Fuel Treatments, and Wind Alignment

The location an intensity of the fuel treatments used to protect the real and resource values occurring near Warm Lake were influenced by the prevailing winds and how they interacted with the topography (e.g., slope angle and aspect, drainage orientation, and their juxtaposition). For example, prescribed fires were most often used to treat fuels on southerly and westerly aspects and within east to west aligned drainages containing steep side slopes (fig. 6). Several times the location of the Monumental Fire, orientation of the topography, and winds aligned perfectly to produce intense fire. As the fire burned on August 12 and 13 along the east side of Warm Lake, it became established near the mouths of the Warm Lake, Bear, and Camp Creeks. Subsequently, driven by strong westerly winds, the fire burned intensely through the entirety of these drainages (fig. 36). In particular, when the fire burned the Warm Lake Creek drainage, it burned around if not over the YWAM Camp (figs. 22, 23, 24).

Figure 36. The winds blowing from the southwest aligned perfectly with the orientation of the Warm Lake, Bear, and Camp Creek drainages and facilitated intensive fire behavior (A) as the Monumental Fire burned the entirety of these watersheds (B).

Another example of wind and topography aligning occurred on August 17 when the strong southerly winds aligned with the topography of the South Fork of the Salmon River and resulted in intense behavior by the Monumental Fire (fig. 37).

Fuel Treatments and Suppression Activities

Not only did the presence of the fuel treatments directly impact the survivability of the many structures located within the basin, but they also influenced fire suppression strategies and the location of the Incident Command Post (Bull and others 2007). Even before the strategic direction was changed from confinement to point defense, the location and presence of the fuel treatments were integral to the development of the appropriate management response (AMR). Knowing that the fire intensity was most likely going to be low to moderate in the areas where the fuels were treated led to the prioritization of both firefighting resources and specific tactics during the fires. For example, mechanical fuel treatments to the south and west of the Kinney Point summer homes were critical in determining where burnout operations were applied (figs. 18, 19). These treatments had a very positive effect on protection capability of these homes, especially when the Monumental Fire intensely approached on August 13 and 17 (figs. 22, 32, 33). These treated areas, along with those on Kline Mountain, were responsible for markedly decreased fire intensity, which allowed fire crews to easily suppress the many spots that were ignited in the fuel treatments. Often these spot fires were near one of the many summer homes located in the area. The fuel treatment areas, in addition to Warm Lake itself, often provided a safe zone for firefighters as the fire(s) burned.

Figure 37. Winds blowing from the south aligned perfectly with the orientation of the South Fork of the Salmon River (A) and created an intense fire as the Monumental Fire burned to the north and ultimately into areas charred by the North Fork Fire (B).

Within the Paradise Valley summer home vicinity (northeast of Warm Lake), the location and presence of fuels treatment areas also influenced suppression activities (fig. 38). Both hand- and mechanical-fire line constructions used the presence and location of the fuel treatments to determine line locations (fig. 38). Similar to areas along the lake, numerous spots were ignited by the North Fork Fire in the Paradise Valley summer homes, Project Work Camp, and Church Camp fuel treatment areas and they were easily suppressed (fig. 39). As with near the lake, burnout operations could be safely executed where the fuels had been treated. This strengthened protection to that already offered by the fuel treatments to the homes and other buildings in the area.

Figure 38. Burnout operations occurred in the masticated fuels near the Paradise Valley summer homes (A, B) in anticipation of either the Monumental or North Fork Fires approaching. The burn severity (soil and tree) as a result of both fires was less in the areas treated compared to the untreated fuels (C). Note the fire line along the treated fuels.

USDA Forest Service Gen. Tech. Rep. RMRS-GTR-229. 2009

27

Figure 39. Spot fires were readily suppressed (A) in the Baptist Church Camp where the fuels had been treated (B).

Although not as obvious as other examples of how fuel treatments influenced suppression activities, the mechanical treatments located along the Warm Lake Highway influenced fire management. The location of the area where the fuels had been masticated played into the decision to burnout the fuels located between the Two-bit Road and the southeastern perimeter of the North Fork Fire (figs. 25, 26) (Bull and others 2007). Even though this burnout operation was less successful than others at interrupting the progression of the North Fork Fire, the location of the fuel treatment was a determinant in burning the fuels on the morning of August 13. The burnout, in addition to the South Fork of the Salmon River and the area where the fuels were masticated along the Warm Lake Highway, was thought to offer protection

to Knox Ranch as the North Fork Fire approached (Bull and others 2007). If the fire would not have spotted to the south side of the Warm Lake Highway, these areas may have interrupted the fire's incursion into the Knox Ranch (figs. 27-29).

As the Monumental and North Fork Fires quickly increased in size and complexity, and containment, the traditional approach to suppressing wildfires, became unattainable. From July 19 through August 15 the Wildland Fire Situation Analysis (WFSA) prescribed containment as the approach to managing the fires and during this time only, 18% of the fires were contained (Bull and others 2007). Therefore, on August 15, rather than trying to contain the fires, the decision was made to protect values within the area from the fires, or switch to point protection (Bull and others 2007). The areas around Warm Lake where the fuels were treated fit well into this fire management strategy (figs. 6, 8-11).

Fuel Treatments and Fire Behavior

On more than one occasion during the Monumental and North Fork Fires, the fuel treatments and their resulting forest structures and compositions modified the behavior of the fires compared to areas where the fuels were not treated. Fuel composition, moisture content, and structure are major determinants of fire behavior and are easily modified by fuel treatments (Agee 1993; Graham and others 2004; Jain and others 2008). Their disposition, combined with topography, fire locations, and interaction with fuel suppression activities ultimately determines how a fire behaves.

A telling interaction of fuel treatments and fire behavior was observed when the Monumental Fire burned by, and possibly over, portions of the YWAM Camp (figs. 21-24). Fire suppression strategies for the Monumental Fire assumed that the forests previously burned by the Bear Creek Fire (1989) would most likely confine and/or slow the spread of the Monumental Fire (fig. 5) (Bull and others 2007). As such, the fuel treatment area south of Kinney Point on the west side of the lake, and areas burned by the Bear Creek Fire, in combination, led to the burning of the fuels between these locations to further hinder the movement of the Monumental Fire. However, the burning conditions on August 13 overwhelmed the effects that both the fuel treatments and past wildfires had on the fire, as it burned intensely and rapidly spread to the east (figs. 28, 29).

The Monumental Fire burned with such intensity ($\approx$100 to 200-ft flame lengths) that spot fires were ignited on the north side of Warm Lake Creek by embers produced over a mile away (figs. 21, 22). Weather and fuel conditions were such that these spots spread rapidly and over 200 acres were burning within minutes (≈10 minutes). On the opposite slope, the area burned by the Bear Creek Fire of 1989 burned with such intensity that it ignited tree canopies mid-crown and toppled trees within the YWAM Camp (figs. 23, 24). In contrast, even though the fire spread rapidly on the south facing slope immediately to the north of the camp where the surface and ladder fuels had been treated (1996), lower fire intensity was observed (figs. 6, 23). Most likely, if high fire intensity would have occurred on both the north and south side of the YWAM Camp simultaneously, the flaming front would have been continuous across the drainage. Such flaming would have most likely burned the majority, if not all, of the cabins within the camp (figs. 22-24).

Warm Lake's location in relation to the camp also contributed to the YWAM Camp surviving the fire. When flaming fronts pass non-burnable areas such as lakes, rock out-croppings, and in some cases, where fuels have been treated, a fire's continuity can be disrupted. This "eddy effect" is much like the calm water that is present in a stream after water passes around a rock (Finney and others 2003). After a fire passes such an area, even when driven by strong winds such as with the Monumental Fire, it takes time for the fire to regain the same intensity it had before hitting the change in fuels. This eddy effect was noticeable within the meadow and forests immediately to the east of Warm Lake that were minimally impacted by the fire (fig. 35). Monumental Fire crews readily suppressed several spot fires that occurred in this area as the fire was burning intensely to the east.

The Monumental Fire burn area adjacent to the YWAM Camp also illustrates how forests can regenerate and develop after a fire or fuel treatment to create fuels that can burn intensely. The Bear Creek Fire of 1989 burned the north facing slope located to the south of the YWAM Camp leaving abundant dead fuels (fig. 5). The vegetative development over the intervening years (1989 and 2007), in combination with fuels remaining after the 1989 fire, created conditions that facilitated intense fire behavior (figs. 21, 23). This observation illustrates that both fuel treatment longevity and effectiveness are dependent on location, dead and live fuel ratios, and rate, composition, and structure of vegetative recovery (development) (Jain and others 2008).

Kline Mountain, rising 600 ft above the west side of Warm Lake Warm Lake, is a small bluff that separates the lake from the South Fork of the Salmon River (fig. 6). The fuels on its east, south, and west sides were burned in 2006. The Monumental Fire approached the mountain from the south on August 13 and 17, and the North Fork Fire burned the north side on August 14 (figs. 22, 27, 28, 32, 33). The Monumental Fire intensity was highly variable in areas on Kline Mountain where the fuels were treated compared to areas on the west side of the Salmon River where the fuels were not treated and the area was severely burned (fig. 40).

Figure 40. High burn severity to the water's edge was a result of the Monumental Fire intensely burning along the South Fork of the Salmon river on the west side of Kline Mountain (A). In contrast, a mosaic of burn severities occurred directly to the east on Kline Mountain where the fuels were burned in 2006 (B).

USDA Forest Service Gen. Tech. Rep. RMRS-GTR-229. 2009

29

Fuel Treatments and Burn Severity

The mechanical treatments and fire suppression activities conducted on the west side of the lake and near the Paradise Valley summer homes contributed significantly to no loss of structures. Altered fuels on the slope directly adjacent to the YWAM Camp to the north, while less obvious, very likely contributed to the survival of YWAM Camp (figs. 3, 6, 21-24). Similarly, the fuel treatments located near the Forest Service Project Camp, Baptist Church Camp, Warm Lake Camp Ground, and Warm Lake Lodge modified fire behavior and offered suppression opportunities that allowed these areas to stay intact while the North Fork and Monumental Fires burned (figs. 34, 38, 39).

Following camps, lodges, and homes, vegetation is the most cherished structure in a forest. Trees are valued for lumber as well as wildlife habitat, scenery, sense of place, and soil and water protection (DeBano and others 1998; Franklin and others 2002; Monroe and others 2006). A large portion of trees survived in the areas along the west side of the lake where the mechanical fuel treatments were conducted and spot fires were quickly extinguished (fig. 41). When the North Fork Fire burned through the area along the Warm Lake Highway where the fuels were masticated, intense fire behavior occurred (fig. 27). When the fire made its major run, one would have expected all trees in its path to be severely burned and all of the foliage consumed. However, near the center of the treatment area, several trees did survive, as did many small seedlings and lower plants. Although the area was severely burned, the remnant trees and green vegetation within this area will lead to more rapid vegetative recovery compared to adjacent areas where all trees were black (fig. 42).

Figure 41. Contrasting burn severities to soils and trees were noticeable as a result of the Monumental Fire burning into the Warm Lake south mechanical fuel treatment area (A) and an adjacent untreated area (B).

Figure 42. The soils experienced far greater heating (higher burn severity) in areas that were not mechanically treated (A) compared to adjacent areas where they were treated in the Warm Lake Highway mastication unit (B) (see figs. 6, 11).

Soil condition after a wildfire determines how quickly a forest will recover and the quality of the water running from burned lands (Debano and others 1998; Robichaud and others 2003). Vegetation loss increases the potential for both wind and water erosion. The heat of a fire, depending on soil characteristics, often alters the soil's biological, chemical, and physical properties. Reducing and/or altering fuels in proximity to the soil's surface can lessen the amount and duration of the heat impacting the soil (Hungerford and others 1991). In most prescribed fire areas, a mosaic of soil and tree burn severities was left after being burned by either the North Fork or Monumental Fires (fig. 43). In these areas, a large number of trees were often killed and several had their crowns scorched. However, if the needles were not consumed by the fires, they will fall and provide protection and organic matter to the soil, which aids in the forest's recovery (Pannkuk and Robichaud 2003; Robichaud and others 2000) (figs. 43, 44). Similarly, in mechanically treated areas that were burned during burnout operations, the wildfires, or by both tended to have mosaics of soil burn severities (figs. 41, 42, 45).

Figure 43. From a distance (Knox Ranch) (A) and within the forest (B), a variety of burn severities were noticeable within the Reaves Creek and Warm Lake Creek fuel reduction projects after they were burned by the Monumental and North Fork Fires.

USDA Forest Service Gen. Tech. Rep. RMRS-GTR-229. 2009

31

Figure 44. Abundant green trees and minimal soil heating were evident on the east (A) and west (B) sides of Kline Mountain that had been treated with prescribed fire and burned by the Monumental Fire on August 17.

Figure 45. Burn severity to both trees and soils was minimal after burnout operations (A) and subsequent wildfire (B), as exemplified within areas where the fuels were mechanically treated during the Warm Lake south project.

Conclusions

The Forest Service and cooperators spent over $1.6 million treating the fuels near Warm Lake. The treatments were strategically placed to offer protection to the many summer homes and other values at risk to wildfire in the area (figs. 3, 4, 6). As a result, the North Fork and Monumental Fires burned only two rustic buildings. Depending on their veracity and longevity, the fuel treatments disrupted the progress of both the Monumental and North Fork wildfires and influenced the burn severity or what was left after the fires (Jain and Graham 2007; Jain and others 2008). Contrary to what is often expected, the fuel treatments did not stop the progression of either fire and when combined, the fires burned over 150,000 acres (fig. 35).

By modifying the fires' behavior, the fuel treatments presented suppression opportunities that otherwise may not have been available. These opportunities included providing locales to conduct burnouts to locating both hand and machine constructed fire lines (figs. 38, 45). The presence of the Warm Lake Highway mechanical fuel treatment contributed to the decision to keep Incident Command Post in Knox Ranch as the North Fork Fire approached (figs. 27, 28) (Bull and others 2007). Similarly, the mechanical fuel treatments in the Kinney Point area along the west side of the lake were the preferred locations for burnouts and fire line construction, as were the treatment areas near the Paradise Valley summer homes (figs. 19, 38, 45).

The intensity of the North Fork and Monumental Fires, in general, was lower on areas where the fuels had been treated compared to areas where they had not, regardless of whether the burning occurred during a burnout or one of the wildfires (figs. 41, 42, 44, 45). In particular, the mechanical fuel treatments were very effective in creating conditions where surface fires dominated. Because of the lower intensity observed in these areas, they often provided safe zones for firefighters and crews were able to readily suppress the numerous spot fires that often occurred (fig. 39). Wildfire spread rates were not lower in areas where the fuels were treated compared to areas where they were not. For example, the prescribed fire conducted in 1996 along Warm Lake Creek opened the stand and led to the development of a lush herbaceous layer (fig. 6). These fuel conditions were very receptive to ignition and rapid fire spread (figs. 22, 23).

By strategically placing fuel treatments within the basin, their presence and location were instrumental in developing the appropriate management response (AMR) to the wildfires. With large and complex fires such as those exhibited in central Idaho in 2007, point or area protection can become the AMR. As such, the presence and location of fuel treatments were influential in determining which values could be protected. In addition, there was evidence that the mechanical fuel treatments near Warm Lake disrupted the fires' progression through landscapes, much like Finney (2001) and Jain and others (2008) have suggested, although the ultimate size of the fires was not impacted (fig. 35).

Homes and other domestic structures are not the only objects that fuel treatments may protect when a wildfire burns. For example, in most cases where the fuel treatments were burned by suppression crews, wildfires, or both, a mosaic of burn severities to both vegetation and soils was observed (figs. 38-45). Intact soils, in combination with varying amounts of live vegetation, will lead to faster vegetative recovery after a wildfire compared to areas where the soils were damaged (Debano and others 1998). When fires heat soils, depending on the temperature achieved and the soil type, nutrients can be volatized, organic matter consumed, and water repellent layers produced (Hungerford and others 1991). A telling contrast displaying this fire result occurred on the west side of Kline Mountain where the fuels had been treated in 2006. In this area, ½- to ¾-acre patches of soils were minimally impacted by the Monumental Fire compared to the west side of the river where the fuels had not been treated and discolored soils dominated. Needless to say, the vegetation on the east side of the river will recover faster than the vegetation on the west side (fig. 40).

Naturally, the vegetation in most forests does not develop with uniformly spaced plants and species mixes, nor when they burn do they burn in such a way to leave uniform vegetative and soil conditions (Finney and others 2003; Oliver and Larson 1990). For example, the mixed species forests that prevailed on the southerly and westerly aspects within the basin tended to have mixed severity fires that left a variety of vegetative and soil conditions. This outcome was especially evident where the forests had been treated with prescribed fire. Also, the mixed severity of burning by the wildfires was apparent across landscapes, even within the more regularly structured lodgepole pine forests. Again, this mixed outcome was enhanced by the presence of fuel treatments as exemplified by how the North Fork Fire burned through the Warm Lake Highway mastication (figs. 27, 28, 46). These observations suggest fuel treatments that create irregular forest structures and compositions, both within and among stands, tend to produce wildfire resilient forests (Graham and others 2004). In addition, these mixed fuel conditions present a more natural look and feel to forests that many wildlife species and people often favor, and such conditions can be

USDA Forest Service Gen. Tech. Rep. RMRS-GTR-229. 2009

33

Figure 46. A variety of burn severities are noticeable as a result of the North Fork Fire burning on August 14 (A, D). The burnout operations were ineffective (B) at preventing the fire from spotting (C) and making a major run to the east toward Knox Ranch (A, D). Low burn severity is noticeable within the 182 acres where the fuels were masticated in 2004 (E) (see fig. 28). (Bottom photo by Bull and others 2007).

created and maintained through silvicultural treatments (Franklin and others 2002; Graham and Jain 2005).

Forests regenerate and develop in response to a variety of disturbances, including weather, fire, harvesting, insects, and diseases (Oliver and Larson 1990). How fast a forest develops is highly dependent on its biophysical setting; however, the moist and cold forests tend to develop faster than dry forests (Haig and others 1941; Lotan and Perry 1983; Pearson 1950). For example, the

Bear Creek Fire of 1989 burned the north facing slope near the YWAM Camp (figs. 3, 5). In the subsequent 18 years, this cold forest was able to produce sufficient fuels, combined with the remnant dead fuels, to facilitate a very intense wildfire (figs. 21, 23). This outcome illustrates the necessity to revisit and, if necessary, retreat forests to maintain fuel conditions that produce the desired wildfire intensity and burn severity (Jain and others 2008; Graham and others 2004).

While the Monumental and North Fork Fires burned in the Warm Lake Basin, the disposition of surface fuels was a major determinant of how the fires progressed. Minimal independent crown fire was evident in the mechanical fuel treatment areas even as the North Fork Fire made its major run toward Knox Ranch (fig. 46). Tree crowns were scorched and burned by surface fires in areas where the fuels were masticated and by the burning of adjacent untreated fuels. Independent crown fires did burn in the basin, especially when the topography, winds, and fire position aligned perfectly as they did when Warm Lake, Bear, and Camp Creeks burned on the east side of Warm Lake (figs. 20, 21, 36). The way the North Fork and Monumental Fires interacted with fuel treatments, roads, and associated suppression efforts reinforce that treatment location and juxtaposition and the treatment of surface fuels, ladder fuels, and crown fuels (in this order of importance) are major determinants of both wildfire intensity and burn severity (fig. 46) (Agee 1993; Finney 2001; Finney and others 2003; Graham and others 2004; Jain and others 2008; Robichaud and others 2003).

Literature Cited

Agee, J. K.; Wright, C. S.; Williamson, N.; Huff, M. H. 2002. Foliar moisture content of Pacific Northwest vegetation and its relation to wildland fire behavior. Forest Ecology and Management. 167:57-66.

Agee, James K. 1993. Fire ecology of Pacific Northwest forests. Washington, DC: Island Press. 493 p.

Alt, D. D.; Hyndman, D. W. 1989. Roadside geology of Idaho. Missoula, MT: Mountain Press. 393 p.

Boise Dispatch Center. 2007. 2007 wildfire season statistics. Internal Report, Boise National Forest. Boise, ID: USDA Forest Service, Boise National Forest. 4 p.

Brown, J. K. 1974. Handbook for inventorying downed woody material. Gen. Tech. Rep. INT-16. Ogden, UT: U.S. Department of Agriculture, Forest Service, Intermountain Forest and Range Experiment Station. 24 p.

Brown, J. K.; Marsden, M. A.; Ryan, K. C.; Reinhardt, E. D. 1985. Predicting duff and woody fuel consumption in the northern Rocky Mountains. Res. Pap. INT-337. Ogden, UT: U.S. Department of Agriculture, Forest Service, Intermountain Forest and Range Experiment Station. 23 p.

Bull, Dave; Moore Ted; Dougherty, Mike; Dawson, Clint; Gales, Shelby; Payne, Jim; Putnam, Ted; Becker, Stephanie. 2007. Cascade Complex: Three days on the Boise, August 12-14, 2007. Accident Analysis. Ogden, UT: U.S. Department of Agriculture, Forest Service, Intermountain Region. 119 p.

Crane, M. F.; Fischer, W. C. 1986. Fire ecology of the forest habitat types of central Idaho. Gen. Tech. Rep. INT-218. U.S. Department of Agriculture, Forest Service, Intermountain Forest and Range Experiment Station, Ogden, UT. 86. p.

Dale V. H.; Joyce L. A.; McNulty S.; Neilson R. P.; Ayres M. P.; Flannigan M. D.; Hanson P. J.; Irland L. C.; Lugo A. E.; Peterson C. J.; Simberloff, D.; Swanson F. J.; Stocks B. J.; Wotton, B. M. 2001. Climate change and forest disturbances. BioScience. 51(9): 723-734.

DeBano, Leonard F.; Neary; D. G.; Ffolliott, P. F. 1998. Fire: its effect on soil and other ecosystem resources. New York: John Wiley & Sons, Inc. 333 p.

Finney, M. A. 2001. Design of regular landscape fuel treatment patterns for modifying fire growth and behavior. Forest Science. 47: 219-228.

Finney, Mark A.; Bartlette, Roberta; Bradshaw, Larry; Close, Kelly; Collins, Brandon M.; Gleason, Paul; Hao, Wei Min; Langowski, Paul; McGinely, John; McHugh, Charles W.; Martinson, Erik; Omi, Phillip N.; Shepperd, Wayne; Zeller, Karl. 2003. Fire behavior, fuel treatments, and fire suppression on the Hayman Fire. In: Graham, Russell T., tech. ed. Hayman Fire Case Study. Gen. Tech. Rep. RMRS-GTR-114. Ogden, UT: U.S. Department of Agriculture, Forest Service, Rocky Mountain Research Station: 33-180.

Franklin, Jerry F.; Spies, Thomas A.; Van Pelt, Robert; Carey, Andrew B.; Thornburgh, Dale A.; Rae Berg, Dean; Lindenmayer, David B.; Harmon, Mark E.; Keeton, William S.; Shaw, David C.; Bible, Ken; Jiquan, Chen. 2002. Disturbances and structural development of natural forest ecosystems with silvicultural implications, using Douglas-fir forests as an example. Forest Ecology and Management. 155: 399-423.

Graham, Russell T.; Jain, Theresa B. 2005. Application of free selection in mixed forests of the inland northwestern United States. Forest Ecology and Management. 209(1-2): 131-145.

Graham, Russell T.; McCaffrey, Sarah; Jain, Theresa B., tech. eds. 2004. Science basis for changing forest structure to modify wildfire behavior and severity. Gen. Tech. Rep. RMRS-GTR-120. Fort Collins, CO: U.S. Department of Agriculture, Forest Service, Rocky Mountain Research Station. 43 p.

Haig, I. T.; Davis, K. P.; Weidman, R. H. 1941. Natural regeneration in the western white pine type. Tech. Bulletin. No. 767. Washington, DC: U.S. Department of Agriculture. 99 p.

Headwaters Economics. 2007. Idaho wildland urban interface analysis. http://www.headwaterseconomics.org/wildfire/id.php#cht. Bozeman, MT: Headwaters Economics. 5 p.

Heim, Jr. Richard R. 2002. A review of Twentieth-Century drought indices used in the United States. Bulletin of the American Meteorological Society. 83: 1149-1165. http://www.ncdc noaa.gov/oa/climate/research/drought/palmer-maps.

Hungerford, R. D.; Harrington, M. G.; Frandsen, W. H.; Ryan, K. C.; Niehoff, G. J. 1991. Influence of fire on factors that affect site productivity. In: Harvey, A. E.; Neuenschwander, L. F. compilers. Proceedings management and productivity of western-montane forest soils. April 10-12, 1990, Boise, ID. Gen. Tech. Rep. INT-280. Ogden, UT: U.S. Department of Agriculture, Forest Service, Intermountain Research Station: 32-50.

Jain, Theresa B.; Graham, Russell T. 2004. Is forest structure related to fire severity? Yes, no, maybe: methods and insights in quantifying the answer. In: Shepperd, Wayne D.; Eskew, Lane G., compilers. Silviculture in special places: proceedings of the National Silviculture Workshop. September 8-11, 2003, Granby, CO. Proceedings. RMRS-P-34. Fort Collins, CO: U.S. Department of Agriculture, Forest Service, Rocky Mountain Research Station: 217-234.

Jain, Theresa B.; Graham, Russell T. 2007. Relation of forest structure to burn severity: the results. In: Powers, Robert., ed. Restoring fire-adapted forested ecosystems. 2005 National Silviculture workshop. June 6-10, 2005, Lake Tahoe, CA. Gen. Tech. Rep. PSW-GTR-203. Albany, CA: U.S. Department of Agriculture, Forest Service, Pacific Southwest Research Station: 121-156.

Jain, Theresa B.; Graham, Russell T.; Sandquist, Jonathan; Butler, Matthew; Brockus, Karen; Frigard, Daniel; Cobb, Davis; Han, Han-Sup; Halbrook, Jeff; Denner, Robert; Evans, Jeff. 2008. Restoration of Northern Rocky Mountain moist forests: integrating fuel treatments from the site to the landscape. In: Deal, Robert, ed. Integrated restoration efforts for harvested forest ecosystems; May 7-10, 2007, Ketchikan, AK. Gen. Tech. Rep. PNW-GTR-733. Portland, OR: U.S. Department of Agriculture, Forest Service, Pacific Northwest Research Station: 147-172.

USDA Forest Service Gen. Tech. Rep. RMRS-GTR-229. 2009

35

Kent, Brian; Gebert, Krista; McCaffrey, Sarah; Wade; Calkin, David; Martin, Ingrid; Schuster, Ervin; Martin, Wise Holly Bender; Alward, Greg; Kumagai, Yoshitaka; Cohn, Patricia J.; Carroll, Matt; Williams, Dan; Ekarius, Carol. 2003. Social and economic issues of the Hayman Fire. In: Graham, Russell T., tech. ed. Hayman Fire Case Study. Gen. Tech. Rep. RMRS-GTR-114. Ogden, UT: U.S. Department of Agriculture, Forest Service, Rocky Mountain Research Station: 315-396.

Lewis, James G. 2005. The Forest Service and the greatest good: a centennial history. Durham, NC: Forest History Society. 286 p.

Lotan, J. E.; Perry, D. A. 1983. Ecology and regeneration of lodgepole pine. Agric. Handb. No. 606. Washington, DC: U.S. Department of Agriculture. 51 p.

Monroe, Martha C.; Nelson, Kristen C.; Payton, Michelle. 2006. Communicating with homeowners in the interface about defensible space. In: McCaffrey, Sarah, tech. ed. The public and wildland fire management: social science findings for managers. Gen. Tech. Rep. NRS-1. Newtown Square, PA: U.S. Department of Agriculture, Forest Service, Northern Research Station: 99-110.

National Interagency Fire Center. 2008. Wildland fire statistics. Boise, ID: USDA Forest Service and USDI Bureau of Land Management. http://www.nifc.gov/fire_info/fire_stats.htm.

Natural Resources Council of Maine. 2008. Public land ownership by state. http://www.maineenvironment.org/documents/publiclandownership.pdf. Augusta, ME: Natural Resources Council of Maine. 3 p.

Natural Resource Conservation Service. 2003. SNOTEL (SNOwpack TELemetry). Portland, OR: U.S. Department of Agriculture, Natural Resources Conservation Service. www.wcc nrcs.usda.gov. 2 p.

Natural Resource Conservation Service. 2008. Big Creek Summit SNOTEL site. Portland, OR: U.S. Department of Agriculture, Natural Resources Conservation Service. http://www.wcc nrcs.usda.gov/snotel/snotel.pl?sitenum=338&state=id.

Oliver, C. D.; Larson, B. C. 1990. Forest stand dynamics. New York: McGraw-Hill Inc. 467 p.

Pannkuk, C. D.; Robichaud, P. R. 2003. Effectiveness of needle cast reducing erosion after forest fires. Water Resource Research. 39(12): 1333, doi:10.1029/2003WR002318.

Pearson, G. A. 1950. Management of ponderosa pine in the southwest as developed by research and experimental practice. Monograph 6. Washington, DC: U.S. Department of Agriculture, Forest Service. 218 p.

Radeloff, V. C.; Hammer, R. B.; Stewart, S. I.; Fried, J. S.; Holcomb, S. S.; Mckeefry, L. J. F. 2005. The wildland-urban interface in the United States. Ecological Applications. 15(3): 799-805.

Rauscher, Michael H.; Hubbard, William G. 2008. Forest encyclopedia network (FEN). http://www.forestencyclopedia net. Atlanta, GA: USDA Forest Service, Southern Research Station, Asheville, NC and, Southern Regional Extension Forestry, Athens, GA. 564-564 p.

Robichaud, P. R.; Byers, J. L.; Neary, D. G. 2000. Evaluating the effectiveness of postfire rehabilitation treatments. Gen. Tech. Rep. RMRS-GTR-63. Fort Collins, CO: U.S. Department of Agriculture, Forest Service, Rocky Mountain Research Station. 85 p.

Robichaud, P. R.; MacDonald, L.; Freeouf, J.; Neary, D.; Martin, D.; Ashmun, Louise. 2003. Postfire rehabilitation of the Hayman Fire. In: Graham, Russell T. tech. ed. Hayman Fire Case Study. Gen. Tech. Rep. RMRS-GTR-114. Ogden, UT: U.S. Department of Agriculture, Forest Service, Rocky Mountain Research Station: 293-313.

Steele, R.; Pfister, R. D.; Ryker, R. A.; Kittams, J. A. 1981. Forest habitat types of central Idaho. Gen. Tech. Rep. INT-114. Ogden, UT: U.S. Department of Agriculture, Forest Service, Intermountain Forest and Range Experiment Station. 138 p.

U.S. Department of Agriculture, Forest Service. 2003. Final forest plan revision Boise National Forest. Ogden, UT: U.S. Department of Agriculture, Forest Service, Intermountain Region. 4 chapters and appendices.

WRCC, Western Regional Climate Center. 2008. Idaho climate summaries. Western Regional Climate Center. http://www.wrcc.dri.edu/summary/climsmid html.